Pies
~ and ~
Tarts
~ with ~
Heart

First published in the United States of America in 2013 by
Quarry Books, a member of
Quayside Publishing Group
100 Cummings Center
Suite 406-L
Beverly, Massachusetts 01915-6101
Telephone: (978) 282-9590
Fax: (978) 283-2742
www.quarrybooks.com

10 9 8 7 6 5 4 3 2 1

ISBN: 978-1-59253-846-1

Digital edition published in 2013
eISBN: 978-1-61058-773-0

Library of Congress Cataloging-in-Publication Data available

Design: Rita Sowins / Sowins Design
Photography: Paul Runyon

Printed in China

Pies
and
Tarts
with
Heart

Expert Pie-Building Techniques for 60+ Sweet and Savory Vegan Pies

DYNISE BALCAVAGE

Quarry Books
100 Cummings Center, Suite 406L
Beverly, MA 01915

quarrybooks.com • craftside.typepad.com

Contents

* Introduction *

I was born on "pi" day: 3.14, also known as March 14. Although math has never been my forte, I am pretty darn good at baking pies.

It seems every time I read about pies, writers impart picture-perfect childhood memories: rolling out dough with an endlessly patient grandma—who of course is wearing a flour-dusted, red gingham apron; candle-shop smells wafting from the oven; perfectly formed pies cooling on country windowsills while a veritable trail of glittery steam vents in curlicues against an impossibly blue sky.

Sadly, I have no such childhood memories. (Anticlimactic, I know.) We were, quite simply, a family of cake and cookie creators, not pie bakers. In fact, the only pies I honestly recall tasting during my childhood were Tastykakes, a Philadelphia brand, and Sara Lee's. I liked them, but I preferred my family's homemade cakes and cookies.

Fast forward to my early twenties, just a few years after the untimely death of my mom. I became increasingly interested in the concept of self-reliance. Around this time, I happened upon the joy of baking pies and of cooking in general. I didn't have an "aha" pie moment, but after I figured out how easy and modular it was, I do recall turning out all kinds of pies with abandon: apple, pumpkin, blueberry, pecan, and even a pumpkin pie made with silken tofu—long before I was vegan—a variation of which I still make regularly (see page 53). People loved my pies, which, of course, inspired me to make them often and to get more creative with my recipes.

What did I like about making pies? I'm a big-picture kind of girl, which is why I usually consider myself a better cook than a baker. I know so many people who are great with details, precise measurements, and records. They have the patience to follow recipe directions and because of this, obtain absolutely consistent results. These are the cake bakers. I'm more of the ad-lib kind of cook—better at doing things by instinct and on the fly.

Which is why pie making agrees with me. Pies are less persnickety to bake than cakes, and they're much more forgiving. You have a bit of wiggle room to express yourself, whether it's by adding an exotic filling "flourish" or an avant-garde cutout design on your pie top. Plus, you don't have to sift the flour!

Baking pies is part art and part sport. In some ways, it's a game of wits because you need to be poised to react—to the ingredients, the weather, and even your cranky old oven. If the peaches are super juicy, for example, you might need to cut back on water-drawing ingredients, such as salt. If the weather is humid or rainy, you may need to add less water to the dough. If your apples are tart, you may need to add more sweetener.

The culinary nerd in me enjoys this. I like the fact that, despite my best efforts, it is unlikely that any two of my pies will taste exactly the same.

Which brings me back to pi, the number. One thing I do know about math is that pi goes on and on and on, and its decimal representation neither ends nor repeats. In 2006, Akira Haraguchi of Japan recited pi to more than 100,000 decimal places, shattering the old record. The process took him sixteen-plus hours.

By the same token, pies go on and on. I doubt people will ever stop baking pies—and that any two homemade pies will ever taste alike.

I hope this book gives you the information and the inspiration to turn out magnificent plant-based pies, done your way.

About the Icons ⌐

Throughout this book, you'll see a series of icons designed to help you quickly skim the recipes.

 GF: Gluten-free*

 Fast: Make this pie in less than 30 minutes

 Low-Fat: Pies are fattening! But these pies contain less fat than average

 Kid-Friendly: Recipes that especially appeal to kids

 Raw: Recipes made entirely from raw ingredients

 No-Bake: Recipes that do not require baking

* Gluten-Free Note

Many of these recipes can easily be made gluten-free by substituting gluten-free ingredients. But if you are gluten-sensitive or gluten-intolerant, you probably know that it's not quite that simple because gluten is insidious. This sneaky ingredient can lurk in even seemingly innocent foods, including some soy sauces and curry powders! So when making something gluten-free, please be sure to scrutinize your food labels and purchase only groceries that are labeled gluten-free.

* Chapter 1 *

Before You Get Rolling: Getting Started

WHAT DO RUNNING AND PIE BAKING HAVE IN COMMON? Simplicity. I love the minimalism of running: you only need a good pair of shoes and some running clothes. The same is true for pie baking: it does not entail loads of fancy equipment or rely on exotic ingredients. Chances are, you probably have just about everything you need on hand in your kitchen as you venture on your pie-baking journey. On the other hand, if you're a connoisseur or gadget freak, there are plenty of options to satisfy your appetite for variety.

(clockwise): gluten-free flour blend, regular flour, cornmeal, xantham gum, cornstarch, and nutritional yeast

Stocking Your Pie-Making Pantry

You'll need a few staples before you start creating your pie. Here's my two cents on pie-baking ingredients.

FLOURS

Flours make up the pie's foundation. Experiment with the mix and taste that you like the best.

♣ **Unbleached all-purpose flour:** All-purpose flour has the perfect amount of gluten needed to create flaky, stretchy crusts. Frankly, pies taste best when they are made with 100 percent all-purpose flour. Because I know it's a health no-no, I usually mix half all-purpose flour with half whole wheat pastry flour, if only to feel virtuous. For me, it's a happy medium of healthy and tasty.

Eating all-purpose flour is not optimal for our health, but I say, "Everything in moderation, including moderation." So if you're trying to impress a date with your baking abilities or if you are bringing a pie into hostile, vegan-unfriendly territory, I suggest using all-purpose flour.

♣ **Spelt flour:** Spelt is a grain in the wheat family. I like it because of its neutral taste and superior nutrition profile; it generally has fewer calories and more protein than wheat flour does. For pie baking, choose white spelt, as opposed to whole-grain spelt, which has a stronger, "earthier" taste. You can also mix some in with all-purpose flour.

♣ **Whole wheat pastry flour:** The texture of whole wheat is a bit heavier and grainier than that of all-purpose flour. But it's healthier, so as I said, I usually mix half and half.

♣ **Gluten-free flour:** There are many brands of premixed gluten-free flours, usually made from some combination of sorghum flour, tapioca flour, potato starch, and sometimes even garbanzo and/or fava bean flour! Gluten helps your dough stick together and get stretchy, so when using gluten-free flours, you'll need to add xanthan gum to the mix to get the job done. (There's a way around everything, right?)

(clockwise): pistachios, macadamia nuts, cashews, peanuts, walnuts, and almonds

NUTS

Almonds, walnuts, pistachios, macadamia nuts, pecans, and more make a wonderfully rich and healthy filling. You can also use nuts to make an easy, earthy nut crust (see page 36). Choose nuts that look fresh and unblemished—smell and taste them if you can. Your nose will know. If they smell "off," or like varnish, they probably are past their prime. Because nuts spoil quickly, buy only what you need and store leftovers in the refrigerator to prolong their usefulness.

FATS

Fats are such an important pie crust ingredient. They not only add flavor to the crust, but they also melt to create the signature "flakes."

❖ **Earth Balance:** This is a nonhydrogenated vegan butter substitute, aka vegan margarine. The flavor is rich and "buttery," and it works well in pie crusts. It melts somewhat more quickly than does shortening, though, so I often mix half Earth Balance with half shortening.

❖ **Vegetable shortening:** Shortening tastes neutral, which can be good or bad. But it tends to stay cold and solid longer than Earth Balance does.

❖ **Oils:** Lots of people love oil-based crusts, but I am not a fan; they are too tough for my taste. But if you are concerned about processed fats, by all means, give oils—such as olive oil and coconut oil—a try in your crusts. I recommend chilling them first and then re-chilling the dough for at least a few hours before rolling.

❖ **Vegan cream cheese:** I use vegan cream cheese to thicken fillings in many of my recipes. I also like the fact that it has a neutral taste. Look for a nonhydrogenated version. My brand of choice is Galaxy. It's made with coconut, melts very easily, and has the added benefit of being gluten-free.

FRUITS AND VEGETABLES

Shop seasonally. Shop locally. I know you're probably tired of hearing this mantra, but really, it's the best way to sniff out produce at the height of its flavor for the lowest price—with the lowest impact on mama earth as a special bonus.

I live near the Reading Terminal Market, a large food market in Philadelphia, where I continually find pie inspiration in several of the produce stands. I might spy a succulent bushel of peaches, just begging to be sliced up and made into a pie. Or luscious, fresh-picked raspberries and blue-berries screaming at me from the fruit stall. Sometimes, it's best to let the fruit choose which pie you'll make, instead of deciding on a recipe and then going out to find the fruit.

Joining a CSA (community-supported agriculture) share is another wonderful option for both fruits and vegetables. You pay a fee, usually for a season at a time, up front. Then once or twice a week, you either pick up or receive a delivery of fresh fruits and/or vegetables from a local farm. I've found that participating in CSA shares also helps me expand my culinary repertoire by forcing me to cook with ingredients that I normally would not buy.

For fruit pies, especially berry pies, you can also substitute frozen fruit—a handy idea in February when you can't take another day of snow and simply must have a mixed-berry pie or you will die. Frozen fruit can be a bit more watery than fresh, so you might need to adjust and add extra thickener.

THICKENERS

These are some of the most common thickeners used in my recipes. They are more or less inter-changeable, but I use flour and cornstarch mostly, because I am cheap … er … frugal.

✤ **Arrowroot:** This is an inexpensive thickener made from the powdered root of the obedience plant. (The anarchist in me wants to bypass arrowroot for this reason.)

✤ **Cornstarch:** This is finely ground corn flour. Look for a non-GMO (genetically modified organism) brand. Cornstarch is my go-to thickener.

✤ **Kudzu:** This wonderful, natural thickener is made from the root of the kudzu plant, but oy, it's expensive.

✤ **Flour:** Flour is a respectable thickener, and you can't get any cheaper. But it's thicker than some of the other thickening options, so a little goes a long way.

Some sweeteners to keep on hand
(clockwise): white sugar, agave nectar,
maple syrup, and brown sugar

SWEETENERS

A dizzying array of sweeteners is available. For pie-baking purposes, though, I rely on these basic five:

❖ **White sugar:** White sugar is the most common pie sweetener and with good reason. It's cheap, dissolves easily, and gets the sweetening job done. Most white sugar is made from sugar cane, but some is created from the sugar beet.

Not all white sugar is vegan. Most of the big-brand 5-pound bags you see in large grocery stores are processed with bone char, the ground-up bones of slaughtered cows. This whitens the sugar and helps separate it.

Personally, I love the champagne blonde color of vegan sugar. And it smells deliciously stickysweet, like a scented candle from a fancy shop, but better. So you can imagine how much better natural sugar makes your baked goods taste. Most processed/non-vegan sugar is odorless, a fact that I find disturbing because a plant food should have a scent.

You can find vegan sugar at Whole Foods and most health food stores. An added bonus is that it's usually fair trade. At press time, Whole Foods (365 Brand), Jack Frost, Hain Organic, and Florida Crystals produce vegan sugars.

If you prefer a less processed form of white(-ish) sugar, look for beet sugar or date sugar.

❖ **Brown sugar:** Brown sugar is simply white sugar that has been colored with molasses, so it has a deeper, slightly caramelly flavor and comes in gorgeous tawny hues. Both light and dark brown are available. Again, look for vegan brands or vegan varieties like maple, turbinado, moscavado, and demerara.

❖ **Maple syrup:** The indigenous North Americans first made Maple syrup—the sweet sap of the sugar, black or red maple tree. In the United States and Canada, we are fortunate to be able to enjoy this amber treat year long and at a relatively low cost. In other countries, it is considered somewhat exotic. I like its quiet caramel flavor and the fact that it's less processed than white sugar.

In Canada, where maple syrup flows from the tap, syrups are graded in a range of colors: extralight, light, medium, amber and dark. In the U.S., we keep it down to three grades: light, medium, and dark amber. All grades taste wonderful, so I don't get too hung up on specifics. But typically, the darker syrups are used for baking, while the lighter ones are used to top pancakes and waffles.

❖ **Molasses:** Molasses is a thick, sludge-like sweetener that is made from the sugar cane. Its name is derived from the Portuguese word *melaço,* which itself is derived from *mel,* the Latin word for "honey." Personally, I think it's a stretch. Molasses is sweet, but it's also got an earthy, metallic taste. Coincidentally, it is very high in iron and calcium. Molasses is the deep flavor foundation of shoofly pie. Look for unsulfured molasses—it does not contain sulfur dioxide, a preservative.

Make your own brown sugar:

Mix one cup (200 g) of white sugar with 2 T (40 g) molasses.

❖ **Agave nectar:** This sweet syrup is produced from the agave plant, the same succulent wonder that gives us tequila. It can be used interchangeably with maple syrup, though the flavor is different—lighter and fruitier.

Like maple syrup, there are several varieties of agave: light, dark and amber, which range in flavor intensity from light to dark. I almost always prefer the dark, but then again, I enjoy intense flavors. Agave nectar is generally considered a raw food, since it's processed at temperatures below 188°F (87°C), but if you're a raw food purist, look for a brand specifically labeled as "raw."

OTHER INGREDIENTS

Be prepared! Having these additional ingredients on hand is helpful.

❖ **Baking soda:** If you are trying to limit your sugar intake, using baking soda can help you cut down on the amount of sugar called for (a handy little tip I read in *The Tightwad Gazette*, by Amy Dacyczyn). Add ¼ to ½ teaspoon to your filling, and you can reduce the sugar in the recipe.

Types of chocolate: chips, chunks, and two types of cocoa: regular and raw cacao

❖ **Phyllo dough (also called filo):** This thin pastry is often used for Middle Eastern and Greek desserts, but it makes a fabulous tart base. Many people are afraid to work with it, but there's no need. Just cover what you are not using with a damp tea towel, and it won't dry out.

❖ **Puff pastry:** Puff pastry is a rich, ready-made crust and because it is jam-packed with fat, it puffs when you bake it. I love it because it's such a versatile tart base. You can top it with practically anything you like and voilà—you have a gorgeous dish, sure to produce lots of oohs and aahs.

❖ **Salt:** I usually use sea salt or kosher salt in my pies. But with the gourmet salt craze you can really get creative and add flavored salts to complement or contrast with your pies and/or crusts. When I spoke at the Vida Vegan Conference in Portland, Oregon, my friend and fellow cookbook author Julie Hasson took me and Bryanna Clark Grogan (another friend and fellow cookbook author) to a store called The Meadow, which sells only salt and chocolate. They offered every imaginable variety and color of salt. It was a real education. I brought home a few unique bottles, including a bottle of chocolate salt, which I have since used in chocolate-centric pies and baked goods (see www.atthemeadow.com).

❖ **Vegan sour cream:** If you don't feel like making your own topping, vegan sour cream is a thick, rich pie topper that goes especially well with fruit pies, such as apple and pumpkin, and with creamy, decadent pies.

❖ **Xanthan gum:** This ingredient is made from an itty-bitty microbe called *Xanthomonas campestris*. But don't let that put you off: it's a godsend for gluten-sensitive and allergic folks because it adds heft and helps bind gluten-free flours. You might recognize the name because it's commonly used to thicken sauces, ice creams, and salad dressings.

Food Notes

Plant-based. Herbivorous. Vegan. No matter what you call them, animal-free pies are tasty, compassionate pies. And if you're going to the trouble of making a pie, why not use the best ingredients?

PARLEZ-VOUS VEGAN?

Actions speak louder than words, but words are extremely powerful. Sadly, women tend to dilute this power by using qualifiers when speaking and writing much more frequently than men do. We tend to pose things as questions to get consensus ("It's blue, don't you think?") rather than making assertive statements ("It's blue, dammit."). We also water down statements with words connoting uncertainty, such as "maybe," "perhaps," etc. ("Perhaps it's blue.") Don't even get me started on "like" and "you know."

This is why I'm not a fan of tacking the word "vegan" in front of every recipe or food item. Although "vegan" is technically an adjective, in omnivorous circles, it has also become a qualifier. It quietly implies an inferior product—not to vegans, but to the rest of the world. It's a PR issue. Hearing a cake called "Vegan Red Velvet Cake" bothers me as much as hearing an artist described as a "female artist" or a politician described as an "African-American politician."

This is why I'm skipping the word *vegan* when possible concerning ingredients. When I use the word *sugar*, I mean plant-based sugar—sugar that has not been processed with bone char or other animal products. Ditto for *milk*. You can use any type of nondairy milk you like: soy, flax, coconut, almond, hemp, oat—unless I specify a certain kind. Same goes for chocolate and margarine—they're all plant based, without hydrogenated oils, please.

GOOD STUFF IN, GOOD STUFF OUT

I am not a brand-name kind of girl. If you came into my kitchen and did a pantry raid, you'd find many generic products and grains, nuts, and flours from the bulk bins. But I am loyal to a handful of brand-name products because of their superior taste and performance in recipes.

* Earth Balance is the only vegan margarine I use.
* When playing the stock market, Better Than Bouillon No-Chicken Stock is my go-to broth.
* I have two preferred brands of olive oil, which I think impart lots of flavor for the price: Colavita Private Selection, Frut-tato and 365 Brand (Whole Foods) Cold-Processed Unfil-tered Italian Olive Oil, which comes in a can.
* Vegenaise is the only vegan mayonnaise I will use. Recent-ly, I've fallen in love with their Reduced Fat version, which to me tastes exactly like the full-fat version.
* When it comes to dark chocolate, many excellent brands are available. I prefer Valrhona and Guittard, ideally 65 percent cocoa or higher.
* I only use sea salt or kosher salt.

> ### TartSmart:
> ## Pie
> A baked dish with a crust bottom. Usually made from pastry dough but can also be made from cookies, nuts, or other foodstuffs. Taller than a tart—usually about 2-inches (5 cm) high—and may have a pastry top, crumble top, or no top.

Equipment Notes

You only need a few basic pieces of equipment to make a pie, but there are many different options to choose from.

ROLLING PINS

There are so many types of rolling pins available. Choosing one is truly a matter of personal preference.

❖ **Wood:** I prefer wooden, French tapered rolling pins, also called rods. They are inexpensive, and I think the easiest to work with: you have more control when you are not wrestling with a handle. In fact, whenever I use a rolling pin with a handle, I simply ignore the handles and just roll the dough with the "pin" part.

❖ **Marble:** A definite advantage, besides the aesthetics factor, is that marble pins stay cold. You can also place them in the refrigerator to make them even colder. I used to have a marble rolling pin. Although it looked beautiful, it was much too heavy for rolling out pie crusts.

❖ **Stainless steel:** Like marble, this pin also stays cold and can be chilled. Plus, there's the obvious cool factor—many people would like their rolling pins to match their stainless steel appliances. These can be heavy, but on the plus side they are among the easiest to clean.

❖ **Glass:** Here's another cool cat. Many contain a chamber that you can actually fill with cold water and chill in the fridge. They're pretty, too. But condensation happens. When the cold pin hits the warm air, your dough might become riddled with water droplets—which can be good or bad for your dough, depending on the weather. (I don't own one, because I am certain I would drop it and it would shatter.)

❖ **Nonstick:** I've salivated over these online. I love anything nonstick. They come in both rod and roller form. It's on my Christmas list.

PIE PANS/DISHES

These are the very foundation of your creations! Most pie pans measure 9 inches (23 cm) in diameter by about 2 inches (5 cm) high. You can also buy special deep-dish pie pans, which create bigger, more typical diner-style pies. There's a pie for every budget (or lack thereof): you can spend anywhere from $3 for garden-variety metal pans to upward of $55 for fancy French ceramic pans.

❧ **Glass:** Lots of people dislike glass pans, but a 9-inch (23 cm) glass pie pan is my weapon of choice. It works for me. A big upside is that, while the pie is baking, you can peek underneath to see whether your crust is browning properly. Another upside is that they clean up beautifully in the dishwasher.

❧ **Aluminum pie tins:** These are a tried-and-true favorite. I have a 9-inch (23 cm) pan, and it gets the job done. I find that aluminum browns the crust evenly and is fairly easy to clean up.

❧ **Nonstick:** Nonstick surfaces are a plus when it comes to both serving and cleaning up. But be careful not to damage the surface when you are cutting into your pie.

❧ **Ceramic:** These lovely pans come in a variety of colors and edges (fluted, stamped), and they dress up even a not-so-perfect crust. But the downside is they can be hard to clean and easy to break or crack.

❧ **Tart pans:** A variety of metal tart pans are available—square, round, oval, rectangular. Some come with removable bottoms. I recommend having one 10-inch-ish (25 cm) tart pan in the shape of your choice.

❧ **Mini tart pans:** I use minis for all my raw pies, which typically serve one or two people. You can divide up a regular pie or tart among several minis. You'll just need to adjust the baking time.

❧ **Muffin tins and mini muffin tins:** These are great for making single-serving pies.

❧ **Paper:** Gourmet shops, such as Fante's here in Philadelphia, sell pretty tart pans made from stiff paper. These are inexpensive and make your tarts look like you bought them in a fancy bakery. This option is great when making tarts as gifts.

❧ **Foil:** These recyclable pans are another good option for gifts. Crusts turn out respectably crispy in these humble little numbers. Save the ones you get from store-bought pies. (Yes, I do indulge once in a while!) They're indispensable when you are making pies to give as gifts.

OTHER INDISPENSABLE EQUIPMENT

Here are some other items that you'll want to have in your kitchen to turn out perfect pies.

Pastry cutter: Pastry cutters help you cut the flour into the fat, and they look a bit like a deconstructed wire whisk. I resisted buying one for years and instead relied on the "two knives" method of cutting in the fat (which I am not even bothering to explain in this book because I don't recommend it). But acquiring a pastry cutter changed my life. There are many available. Try holding a few and choose one that feels good in your hand.

Food processor: This is an indispensable appliance for both making crusts and mixing certain fillings to achieve a creamy consistency. There are many beautiful processors on the market. Although I have been coveting a red KitchenAid for years (I love red), I've had my Regal La Machine for the past thirty years and it's still going strong. At this point, it looks like we might be together for life. That said, do your research before buying and figure out where you will store it.

❖ **Cookie/baking sheet:** Placing your pie on a cookie sheet catches any filling spillover, saving you tons of cleanup time. It can also help your crust brown more evenly on the bottom. Plus, if you are the real do-it-from-scratch type, you'll need several to bake cookies for cookie pie crusts. Chances are you have more than a few of these stashed in your kitchen.

❖ **Oven thermometer:** Oven temperatures can make or break (literally) a pie crust. Make sure your oven temperature is correct. If it saves two or three under- or overcooked pies from the trash bin, this $10 investment will pay for itself.

❖ **Pie weights:** These tiny bead-like weights are indispensable when "blind baking" a crust. They keep the crust from bubbling and buckling, and the resulting indentations create a pretty polka-dot pattern on the inside bottom crust (which, sadly, no one but you will see). If you make a lot of pies, you will want to invest in a set of ceramic or metal weights; I have ceramic weights. If you only occasionally dabble in blind baking, then a bag of dried beans will get the job done.

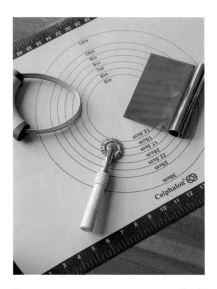

Pastry cutter, pastry scraper, pastry wheel, and pastry mat

Tiny cookie cutters

❖ **Pie vents:** These are also called pie birds. Although you might think that these cute little tchotchkes are simply accessories, they actually serve a purpose and help vent steam from the pie, via the bird's open mouth. Some people collect pie birds. Keep your eyes open for vintage birds and other pie-venting critters when cruising yard sales and flea markets.

❖ **Spatulas:** I'm a sucker for silicone spatulas. They're useful for grabbing that last bit of filling from a bowl. Because I use several a day, I keep my entire collection—ranging from teeny to extra large—in a little French ceramic pitcher on the shelf near my oven so they are always within reach. Choose spatulas in bright, cheerful colors in various sizes—mini, small, medium, and large. You don't have to spend a mint, either. Your local dollar store will probably carry a variety.

❖ **Measuring cups and spoons:** I find that I never seem to have enough, so I am constantly on the lookout. The collapsible versions are especially nice if, like me, you work in a city kitchen or are pressed for space.

❖ **Pastry or Silpat mat:** You can roll out your dough on waxed or parchment paper, a marble countertop, or a stainless steel chef's table, but I find a pastry or Silpat mat makes the entire rolling process much more pleasurable. I have a large Silpat mat that has several measured pie and cake rounds (9 inches [23 cm], 10 inches [25 cm], and so on) drawn on the mat, so it takes the guesswork out of rolling the dough to fit your pan.

Pie weights

Pie vents, or pie birds

Measuring cups and spoons

Spatulas

❖ **Pastry wheel:** You can use a knife or a pizza cutter in a pinch, but a pastry wheel gives you a nice, slightly scalloped edge, especially useful when creating lattice crusts.

❖ **Pie shields (aka crust shields):** These keep your crust from browning too quickly while baking. If you're all about gadgets, then by all means, buy one. Because I hate clutter, I simply use 2-inch (5 cm) strips of aluminum foil, lightly placed around the crust, to do the same job, if and when needed.

❖ **Waxed paper:** Some of you are lucky enough to have naturally nonstick marble or granite countertops for dough rolling, but many people like to roll out their dough on waxed paper to avoid making a mess. It does make cleanup a breeze.

❖ **Parchment paper:** This makes a good liner for phyllo crusts.

❖ **Pie crust bag:** This is not necessary, but if you are a perfectionist—or are terrified of crust making— this gadget's for you. It's simply a round plastic bag with a zipper, premeasured to encase dough to make an 8- to 9½-inch (20 to 24 cm) pie crust. Simply place your dough ball inside, roll until the dough meets the edges, unzip, and voilà! Out pops a near-perfectly round crust.

❖ **Pastry scraper:** This is useful for cutting fat and for scraping bits of dough off your surface. They come in a variety of materials, but I prefer metal.

❖ **Cookie cutters:** You can use tiny cookie cutters to cut out shapes to vent your double-crusted pies. Williams-Sonoma sells tiny cutters made especially for pie venting, but you can use any wee cutters. Or you can cut your own designs directly into the crust with a knife. If you are of the Martha Stewart ilk, you can also use cookie cutters or sharp knives to cut shapes from the dough, which you can use to decorate the edges.

How to Clean Pie Weights

When the pie weights are cool, place them in a colander. Pick away any straggling bits of dough, swish with dish soap, and rinse until the water runs clear.

* Chapter 2 *

Crust Basics and Recipes

PIE CRUSTS ARE EASIER TO MAKE THAN YOU MIGHT THINK, and as is the case with everything else in life, the more often you make them, the easier it will become. I'm not going to lie, though: making your first pie crust can be a bit stressful, if only because it's uncharted territory and you are not exactly sure of what to do, no matter how many recipe books and cooking shows you've studied. That's because cooking and baking are experiential and tactile experiences. You learn from watching, but you mostly learn from doing—and from the repetition of doing. My grandmother didn't have the Food Network or cookbooks growing up on a farm in Bialystok, Poland, for example. But when she came to this country at age fourteen, she knew her way around a kitchen, thanks to watching her mom cook and helping her. During the Depression, after my grandfather died in the mines, she worked as a cook to support her five kids. And she was known for her food.

So I promise that after you make four or five crusts (sooner, if you are a prodigy), you will have a "light bulb" pie crust moment: the magical instant, when the culinary universe decides to conspire with you and it will all come together. Instead of clumsily fumbling with the mixing, rolling, and crimping, juggling ingredients, dropping utensils, and ending up with more flour on your jeans than on your rolling surface, you will, in that flash, feel like a ballerina in a froufrou apron as you effortlessly turn out crust after crust, tiptoeing around your kitchen leaving a trail of fairy dust wherever you go. Well, maybe not exactly.

But trust me, crust making, like any acquired skill, gets easier—and a little addictive—with practice. Learning to make pie crust is one of the most empowering kitchen tasks I know. If you can make a pie crust, you will never be without dinner, dessert, or a last-minute gift.

Zen and the Art of Pie Crusts ❧

Successful pie crusts are a magical balance of light and might. The best pastry crusts taste light and flaky with an impossibly decadent yet light "melty" texture. At the same time, they need to be substantial enough to house heavy fillings like apples and nuts without falling apart or breaking.

Making the crust seems to be the most intimidating—and, I daresay, even feared—part of the pie-making process. But trust me when I assure you that it's really a simple process once you understand the "whys" behind each of the pie crust steps.

There's a rationale behind each step. And the good news is that you will become more facile with crust making as you practice. After a few pies, you will begin to develop a sense for how much water to add, how thin to roll out the dough, and how to decorate the edges.

CHILL OUT

If you only remember one word about making pie crusts, remember this: COLD! Those little globs of fat melt in the oven, creating the tiny air pockets that create that sought-after flaky crust.

Keeping your ingredients and your tools cold helps prevent the fat from melting before its time. You can't be too careful about this step, particularly if you live in a warm climate or tend to like a warm house (like me). For the same reason, you want to handle the dough as little as possible because your warm hands (and warm heart) will also prematurely melt the fat. Remember these tips:

* Add ice cubes to the water.
* Keep your ingredients cold. I've been known to even pre-chill my flour. Keep it in the freezer if you make pies often or have the room—a filled freezer is more energy efficient, anyway.
* Put your rolling pin, Silpat mats, etc., in the freezer before rolling.
* Always—and I mean *always*—chill your dough in the refrigerator for at least an hour before rolling it out.

My Position on Store-Bought Crusts

I know I should encourage you to always make crusts from scratch. But truth be told, even I, author of a pie cookbook, occasionally purchase store-bought pastry or cookie crusts when I am pressed for time. From an economy standpoint, even if you buy your crusts, your semi-homemade pies will still cost far less and taste at least 50 percent better than a store-bought pie. Please just scrutinize the label and make sure all ingredients are vegan and pronounce-able (no hydrogenated oils, please!). And don't make it a habit!

ROLL WITH IT

A. Lightly flour your rolling surface: a counter, a chef's table, or even your kitchen table lined with waxed paper. Sprinkle about ½ cup (63 g) of flour on one side. You'll need to sprinkle it on the dough as you roll it to prevent sticking.

Remove your dough ball from the refrigerator. If you are making a double crust, only work with one at a time: make one and refrigerate it while you are preparing the other.

B. Flatten the dough ball into a disk, press it down slightly, and lightly flour it and your rolling pin. Gently roll, north to south and then east to west. Some people prefer rolling the dough in a clockwise motion (or counterclockwise, whatever floats your boat).

Try to put even pressure on the pin. Don't fret if you get cracks or if tiny pieces secede from the main crust union and want to go off and start their own nation. Gently patch them back together by moistening the tip of your finger and rubbing the two pieces together. The only parts that will show are the top and the edges of the crust, so don't fuss over fissures in the bottom because your crust needs to hold up to the filling.

C. Once the pie crust is about 1 to 2 inches (2.5 to 5 cm) wider than your pie plate, you're ready to transfer it to your pan. One method is to gently and loosely roll it around your pin and then unroll it into the pie pan.

D. The method I prefer is to simply fold the crust into quarters, place it in the pan, and then unfold it.

PIE CRUST WHYS: STEP BY STEP

Step	Why?	Tips
Add fat (e.g., shortening, margarine)	When baked, the pieces of fat melt and create air pockets, resulting in a signature flaky crust.	Make sure your fat is well chilled.
Cube fat	This makes it easier to complete the next step. It cuts down on the time you'll need to handle the dough.	I pre-dice the fat into pea-size cubes.
Cut fat into flour	This helps create an even distribution of fat "globs," which will result in a flakier crust.	Cut the fat into the flour until it resembles pea- and lentil-size pieces. (Now you understand the method behind the dicing madness.)
Add ice-cold water	This helps flour stick together while keeping fat intact. This is ideal because you want the fat to melt while the pie is baking—and not before—to create air pockets, resulting in a flaky crust. The warmer the water, the more likely your fat will melt, and the less likely your crust will be flaky.	Add ice cubes to the water about 5 minutes before making your crust. Keep it in the freezer until you're ready to mix.
Handle as little as possible	Warm hands melt fat. The less you handle your crust, the more likely your crust will be flaky.	Test tiny balls of dough to see whether they stick together. Don't test the entire dough ball at once.
Refrigerate dough before rolling	You guessed it: this helps keep the fat intact.	Cover it tightly with plastic wrap to prevent it from drying out.
Add sugar to the ingredients just before adding to the pie.	Because sugar coaxes water out of fruit, putting this off until the last minute will help your crust brown more evenly on the bottom. It also helps avoid a soggy or wimpy bottom crust.	Always start with less than the called for amount of sugar and add more to your taste. Taste the filling. If the filling tastes good, that's half the battle.

Finishing School: Decorating Your Pie Crust

There are many different ways to edge your pie, from classic to avant-garde. If you're short on time, you can simply use the tines of your fork to decorate your edges, like grandma did. And if you're in one of those Martha Stewart moods, you can cut one-of-a kind edges from extra pastry dough and create a flourish to rival the Sistine Chapel. I'm giving you all the options. The choice is yours.

 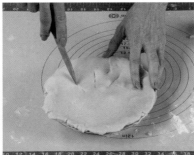 

Make sure to vent your crust.

Mini cutouts

DOUBLE-CRUST PIE TOPS: LET ME VENT!

Before baking your pie, you will need to vent the pie so that steam can escape. You have several options.

✤ **Slits:** This is the easiest. After placing the top crust on the pie and sealing the edges, use a sharp knife to cut evenly spaced slits around the circumference of the pie. Don't be boring! Just because this is the easiest option does not mean your pie has to look ho-hum. You can make a variety of slit patterns and shapes as you cut into the crust: Vs, swirls, slender half-moons, stripes, you name it.

✤ **Cutout vents:** After rolling out the top crust, use tiny cookie cutters (or a knife, if you have a steady hand) to cut shapes from the crust and make a pattern. Some gourmet stores sell mini cutters specifically for this purpose.

✤ **Pie birds:** Steam is vented though the open "mouths" of these cheerful little critters. Just use a sharp knife to cut an X "nest" into the center of your pie. Tuck the birdie in the nest and bake.

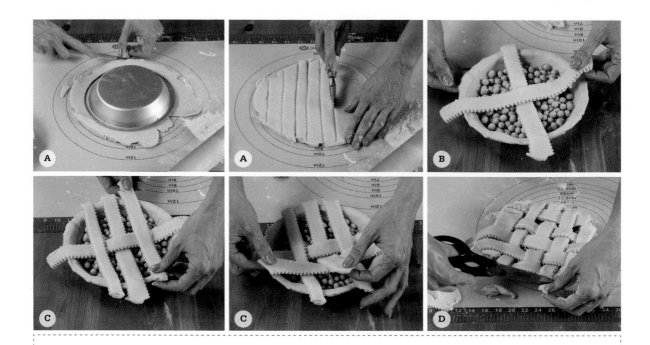

LATTICE CRUSTS

These are my favorite—they're naturally vented! A lattice crust looks fancy-schmancy and is fun to assemble, once you get the hang of it.

A. Roll out your top crust as usual, then cut ¾-inch (2 cm) strips using a very sharp knife, pizza cutter, or pastry edger. Control freaks will use a ruler to create precise strips. Lazy cooks like me will just eyeball it.

B. Make an X across your pie with the longest strips.

C. Lay the next longest strips on either side of one of the axes you just created, "weaving" the dough over and under. Then do the same with the other axis and strips.

D. Trim any extra bulk at the crust edge.

FINISHING TOUCHES

These are optional, but a little extra attention in this department can make your pies look more professional.

❖ **Milk:** Brush your finished crust with nondairy milk. This will make your crust shinier.

❖ **Canola or coconut oil:** Brush your finished crust with oil. Not only will this give your crust a sheen, but it will also impart a hint of richness. If using coconut oil, make sure the oil is melted first—a nonissue if you live in a warm climate.

❖ **Agave or maple drizzle:** Make like Jackson Pollock and drizzle a random, syrupy design over your finished crust. It will brown darker than the rest of the crust and will add another layer of sweetness. I like this option for pies that actually could use more sugar, such as an apple pie using tart Granny Smiths.

❖ **Coarse or turbinado sugar:** After using any of the techniques described above, sprinkle sugar over the top of your pie.

EDGES

Before your finish your edges, you need to cut off any extra dough and create a nice, even finish. Use kitchen scissors or a sharp knife to uniformly trim overhang, leaving about 1 inch (2.5 cm) of extra dough.

A. If you are opting for a forked or cookie-cutout edge, trim right up to the pie plate. If you are opting for a snipped edge, trim to leave about ½ inch (1.3 cm) of extra dough.

B. FLUTED FINISH: This is my go-to finish because it looks fancy, but is even easier than the forked finish. It looks especially nice with fruit pies and rustic pies. Push in dough from the outside of the pan with one index finger and use your other fingers to mold the dough on the inside of the pan around that finger. Repeat until finished, making sure that most of the flutes are even.

C. ARABESQUE FINISH: This is also called a pinched fluted finish, but I've renamed it because it reminds me of the arabesque decorations that adorn mosques. This is the finish you often see on quiches in fancy gourmet takeaways.

Push in the dough from the outside of the pan with one index finger and use your other fingers to mold the dough on the inside of the pan around that finger. Then pinch in the center to make a point. Repeat until finished, making sure that most of the flutes are even.

D. FORKED FINISH: This is grandma's favorite finish. Dip a large fork in flour. Press the dough from the inside of the pan to the outer edge to create decorative stripes. Repeat until finished. You can experiment with the placement of your tine imprints. Try crisscrosses and crosshatches.

E. CUTOUT FINISH (WITH COOKIE CUTTERS OR BY HAND): Whether you are using cookie cutters or cutting the shapes by hand, choose a smallish, uncomplicated shape; cookie cutters with thin sections are more likely to break and do not register visually as effectively as simple shapes do. Some good options include leaves, shapes (circles, squares, diamonds), stars, hearts, shells, and bells. Cut out enough shapes to cover the entire edge. Lightly brush the edge of the crust with water or nondairy milk. Press the shapes onto the crust, slightly overlapping the edges of each shape.

F. CRENELATED FINISH: Use kitchen scissors to snip the edges of the crust at even intervals, spaced about 1 inch (2.5 cm) apart. Bend every other block toward the center of the plate. You can play around with the widths and patterns.

Pie Crust Recipes

Your crust is the very foundation of your pie. It needs to taste neutral enough to avoid competing with your filling ingredients, yet flavorful enough to complement the fillings. Plus it's got to be sturdy enough to house your filling without breaking and hold up to slicing. No pressure there, right? Relax. People have been baking pie crusts for hundreds of years. If they can do it, you can do it.

Think of pie crust, and chances are the simple, all-purpose flour crust comes to mind. Why not? It's comfort food that we were raised on. But there are several crust options and techniques to match every mood, food, and diet. Each individual pie recipe in this book calls for one of these crusts, except for a few recipes that require unique crusts. But in many cases, you can mix and match to create your own unique pies.

Basic Single-Crust Pastry

This basic recipe is the very foundation of most pies. After you make this a few times, you won't even need to consult this cookbook.

Makes one 9-inch (23 cm) crust

½ cup (60 g) whole-wheat pastry flour
¾ cup (94 g) white flour
¼ teaspoon salt
4 tablespoons (56 g) margarine
4 tablespoons (50 g) vegetable shortening
3 to 5 tablespoons (45 to 75 ml) ice-cold water

In a large bowl, mix flour and salt (A).

Dice margarine and shortening (B) and add to the flour, tossing very well so each piece is covered with flour (C).

Using a pastry blender, blend the flour and fats, with the aim of handling the dough as little as possible (D). When the bits are about pea size, start adding water 1 tablespoon (15 ml) at a time, sprinkling evenly onto the dough (E).

Use your hands to toss and gently work, again avoiding manipulating the flour as much as possible (F). (You want to keep the shortening bits intact for a flakier crust). Repeat until the dough just holds together. If the dough feels wet, you have added too much water.

Wrap tightly in plastic wrap (G). Refrigerate for at least 1 hour or overnight .

Roll out as desired. (If leaving dough overnight, give it about 30 minutes to warm up at room temperature before rolling.)

Cutting in Fat with a Food Processor

You can use your food processor to cut in the fat. It's a time-saver, and I do it occasionally, especially when I am making many pies at once. PULSE is the operative word. Never just run your blade or you'll end up with a chewy crust.

Add the flour and salt to the bowl. Whiz to make sure everything is combined and then add your fat cubes, a bit at a time. Pulse the processor until the fat is about pea size. Then transfer to a large bowl, sprinkle in the water, and do the rest by hand. Don't add water in the food processor. Again, this will cut the fat into tiny particles. You need the larger fat globules if you want a flaky crust.

Basic Double-Crust Pastry

Double your pleasure, double your crust! Even if you are making a pie that only requires a single crust, I say you may as well make two at once if you're going to go through the trouble.

Makes two 9-inch (23 cm) crusts

2½ cups (308 g) flour (I use 1 cup
   [120 g] whole wheat pastry flour
   and 1½ cups [188 g] all-purpose
   flour)
½ teaspoon salt
½ cup (112 g) margarine
½ cup (100 g) vegetable shortening
6 to 10 tablespoons (90 to 150 ml)
   ice-cold water

In a large bowl, mix the flour(s) and salt.

Dice the margarine and shortening and add to the flour, tossing very well so each piece is covered with flour.

Using a pastry blender, blend the flour and fats, with the aim of handling the dough as little as possible. When the bits are about pea size, start adding water, 1 tablespoon (15 ml) at a time, sprinkling evenly onto the dough.

Use your hands to toss and gently work, again avoiding manipulating the flour as much as possible. (You want to keep the fat bits intact for a flakier crust.) Repeat until the dough just holds together. If the dough feels wet, you have added too much water.

Wrap tightly in plastic wrap. Refrigerate for at least 2 hours or overnight.

Roll out as desired. (If leaving the dough overnight, give it about 30 minutes to warm up at room temperature before rolling.)

What is Blind Baking?

Some recipes, like the Maple-Laced Caramel-Walnut Pie (page 91), require you to blind bake your pie crust. Blind baking is essentially prebaking the crust either completely or partially *sans* filling. To do this, you need to place some sort of weights in the unbaked crust so that the pie will not buckle. You can use pie weights or even a pound of dried beans. First, put a square of aluminum foil over the bottom of your crust, letting some overlap over the edges, and then pour in the weights.

After baking, you can simply lift up the foil and pour the weights into a colander to wash. If you have ceramic pie weights, please be careful and remove them all before baking the finished pie. Mine are the same color as the crust (genius idea!), and I recently narrowly avoided biting into one and breaking a tooth, or worse yet, accidentally swallowing one.

Gluten-Free Single-Crust Pastry

Gluten makes flour stringy and sticky, so using flours without gluten simply requires a substitute to get the job done. We're using xanthan gum, which is also used as a thickener in many salad dressings and ice creams. Even if you don't have gluten issues, you might still want to give this tasty crust a go. The flavor is subtly nutty.

Yield: Makes one 9-inch (23 cm) crust

1¼ cups (150 g) gluten-free flour
¼ teaspoon salt
¼ to ½ teaspoon xanthan gum
2 tablespoons (28 g) margarine
4 tablespoons (50 g) vegetable
  shortening
3 to 6 tablespoons (45 to 90 ml)
  ice-cold water

In a large bowl, mix the flour, salt, and xanthan gum.

Dice the margarine and shortening and add to the flour, tossing very well so each piece is covered with flour.

Using a pastry blender, blend the flour and fats, with the aim of handling the dough as little as possible. When the bits are about pea size, start adding water, 1 tablespoon (15 ml) at a time, sprinkling evenly onto the dough.

Use your hands to toss and gently work, again avoiding manipulating the flour as much as possible. (You want to keep the fat bits intact for a flakier crust.) Repeat until the dough just holds together. If the dough feels wet, you have added too much water.

Wrap tightly in plastic wrap. Refrigerate for at least 2 hours or overnight.

Roll out as desired. (If leaving the dough overnight, give it about 30 minutes to warm up at room temperature before rolling.) I find that the fork-finished edges are easiest and prettiest with gluten-free crusts.

Pimp Your Pie Crust

Infuse your pie crust with bits of flavor by adding to the flour about ½ to 1 teaspoon of a spice, flavoring, or combination that will complement your filling. Some examples include:
- Cinnamon (apple pie, any stone fruit or berry pie)
- Nutmeg (pumpkin and squash pies, apple pie)
- Cocoa (Chocolate-Bourbon Pecan Pie, page 90)
- Cardamom (Peach Pie with Salted Agave Drizzle, page 44)
- Ginger (Gingered-Pear Pie, page 46; Sweet Potato Pie, page 54)
- Mace (pumpkin and squash pies)
- Vanilla bean scrapings (just about any pie)
- Fruit zest (Key Lime Pie, page 72, and other citrus pies)

Gluten-Free Double-Crust Pastry

GFX2. It sounds like it would be a great name for an independent film convention or a fringe arts festival. But it's just my abbreviation for the gluten-free double crust.

Makes one 9-inch (23 cm) double crust

2½ cups (300 g) gluten-free flour
½ teaspoon salt
½ to 1 teaspoon xanthan gum
4 tablespoons (55 g) margarine
4 tablespoons (55 g) vegetable shortening
6 to 12 tablespoons (90 to 180 ml) ice-cold water

In a large bowl, mix the flour, salt, and xanthan gum.

Dice the margarine and shortening and add to the flour, tossing very well so each piece is covered with flour.

Using a pastry blender, blend the flour and fats, with the aim of handling the dough as little as possible. When the bits are about pea size, start adding water, 1 tablespoon (15 ml) at a time, sprinkling evenly onto the dough.

Use your hand to toss and gently work, again avoiding manipulating the flour as much as possible. (You want to keep the fat bits intact for a flakier crust.) Repeat until the dough just holds together. If the dough feels wet, you have added too much water.

Wrap tightly in plastic wrap. Refrigerate for at least 2 hours or overnight.

Roll out as desired. (If leaving the dough overnight, give it about 30 minutes to warm up at room temperature before rolling.)

Happy Little Scrappies

Have leftover scraps after rolling out your crust? Waste not, want not. Toss them with cinnamon and sugar, dot with margarine, and arrange them on a cookie sheet. Bake while you bake your pie. You can get fancy and use cookie cutters to create perfect little hearts and stars, but I just toss them as is for a more rustic effect. Check after 5 to 10 minutes. Remove from the oven when golden brown. Let cool completely and enjoy.

All-Purpose Cookie Crust

Cookie-type crusts are requisite for certain pies, including Key Lime Pie (using graham crackers, see page 72) and Banana Cream Pie (see page 60). But think beyond the recipe box. Cookie crusts complement the flavors in just about any creamy, chocolaty, or ice cream–based pie. (Sadly, they are not a good crust for fruit pies or gooey nut-based pies; the liquid will turn your crust to mush.) Mix and match fillings and cookie crusts and see what you come up with. As long as you pair like flavors with compatible cookie flavors, you should be fine. Use gluten-free cookies for a gluten-free crust.

Makes one 9-inch (23 cm) crust

1½ cups (150 g) crumbs from dry vegan wafer cookies or graham crackers (try chocolate, gingersnaps, lemon snaps, animal crackers, or just the tops from Oreo-type cookies minus the creamy filling; you'll need about 3 cups [150 g] cookies or crackers to get 1½ cups [150 g] crumbs)

¼ teaspoon salt

4 tablespoons (56 g) margarine

1 teaspoon vanilla extract

Whiz the cookies/crackers and salt together in a food processor until very powdery and fine. Add the margarine and whiz again. Press into your pie pan. That's it!

If you need to prebake, bake for 10 minutes at 350°F (180°C, or gas mark 4).

Smart Cookies

Here are some flavor combination ideas to get you started:
- Gingersnap cookie crust with Pumpkin Pie (page 53) or Sweet Potato Pie (page 54)
- Chocolate cookie crust with Banana Cream Pie (page 60)
- Lemon cookie crust with Lemon Fluff Pie (page 73)
- Chocolate cookie crust with Chocolate Orange Curd Tart (page 76)
- Vanilla cookie crust with No-Bake Coconut Cream Pie (page 69)

Nutty Crust

Nut crusts are a real no-brainer and make a flavorful, sophisticated pie base. I use them in baked, raw, and frozen pies.

Makes one 9-inch (23 cm) crust

2 cups (290 g) nuts (e.g., almonds, pecans, walnuts, macadamia nuts, peanuts, pistachios)

1 to 2 tablespoons (13 to 26 g) sugar

¼ teaspoon salt (omit if nuts are salted)

Optional additions: ½ teaspoon ground spices or other dry enhancers to complement pie flavor (e.g., cinnamon, ground ginger, nutmeg, mace, cocoa powder)

3 tablespoons (42 g) margarine

Whiz the nuts, sugar, salt, and optional additions (if using) together in a food processor to form fine crumbs. Pulse in the margarine.

Press into a pie pan. The goal is to tamp down the crust to about ¼- to ⅛-inch (6 to 3 mm) thick. Use floured fingers or lightly flour the back of a tablespoon to help smooth out the crust. Fill as desired and continue with your raw, baked, or frozen recipe.

Variation

For a raw crust variation, instead of margarine use 3 tablespoons (60 g) raw agave nectar or 4 medjool dates, pitted and soaked in water for about 1 hour. Add when you would add the margarine in the recipe.

Grain-Based Crust

Using cooked grains as a crust for savory pies is a great way to cut the fat and pump up the fiber and nutrients. Most grain crusts lend a pleasant, slightly nutty flavor base to your pie. And grain crusts are economical and a great way to use leftovers; I often use leftover brown rice from my vegan Chinese takeout as crust inspiration.

Generally speaking, the softer the grain when cooked, the easier it is to form into a crust. Millet is my favorite crust base because it's almost dough-like in its pliability. Barley is another winner. Using harder, coated grains like wheat berries and kamut is a bit trickier (but not impossible).

Makes one 9-inch (23 cm) crust

2 cups (about 330 g) cooked grain (e.g., millet, brown rice, quinoa, barley)

2 heaping tablespoons (12 g) nutritional yeast

1 tablespoon (15 g) tahini or other nut butter

Spray a pie pan with cooking spray. Using your hands, mix the grain with the nutritional yeast and nut butter and knead until it becomes malleable. (The amount of time this takes depends on the sturdiness of your grain.) Press into the pan, fill the pie, and bake.

To blind bake, preheat the oven to 375°F (190°C, or gas mark 5). Bake until golden, about 15 to 20 minutes.

Variation

Add finely chopped veggies (e.g., spinach, broccoli, shredded carrot) to the grain as it cooks for a nutritional boost and extra pops of color.

Mashed Potato Pie Crust

We usually think of vegetables as pie filling and not pie bases. But I like to flip things upside down on occasion. Some vegetables, like the potato family, make wonderful savory crust bases. Carbolicious and comforting, mashed potato crusts are economical and an interesting way to transform leftovers into a literal meal base. You can use mashed white potatoes, sweet potatoes, or even mashed turnips or rutabagas— or mix and match.

Makes one 9-inch (23 cm) crust

About 5 potatoes, peeled and baked
   or "nuked"
2 to 3 tablespoons (28 to 42 g)
   margarine
2 to 4 tablespoons (28 to 60 ml)
   nondairy milk (to bind, if needed)
½ teaspoon salt or more, to taste
Freshly ground pepper, to taste

Place the potatoes in a large bowl. Mash with the margarine and milk until creamy. (Use a potato ricer to save time!) Chill in the refrigerator for at least 2 hours.

Place in a lightly greased pan and press into place.

Hash Brown Pie Crust

I love hash browns. Used as a pie crust, these humble potato shreds make a crispy and tasty foundation for savory pies and even vegan quiches: just sprinkle your favorite vegan cheese over the hash browns, top with tofu-quiche filling, and bake. This crust is very easy to make. The hardest part is waiting for the water to drain from the shredded taters!

Makes one 9-inch (23 cm) crust

2 packed cups (220 g) shredded
   potatoes (about 2 large white
   potatoes or 1 large sweet potato)
1 small onion, shredded
¼ teaspoon salt
1½ tablespoons (25 ml) olive oil or
   melted margarine

Place the shredded potatoes and onion in a colander and drain very well. This takes a few hours, but it is an extremely important step. (Soggy taters = soggy crust.) The shreds will turn brown upon oxidation, but this does not matter because they brown as they are baked anyway. After draining, use your hands to gently squeeze out any last bits of water.

Preheat the oven to 425°F (220°C, or gas mark 7).

In a large bowl, using your hands, mix the shreds with the salt and oil. Press into the pan. If you're a perfectionist, you may want to weigh down the crust with another pie pan, but I'm usually too lazy or pressed for time, so I often skip this step.

Bake the crust for about 30 minutes or until golden and crispy.

* Chapter 3 *

Traditional Pies

WHEN IT COMES TO FASHION, IT'S FUN TO HOP
ON TRENDS—like neon colors, crackle nail polish, and pat-
terned tights. They give free spirits like me ample fodder for self-
expression. But it's nice to know, when you're late for work and are
in full-blown fashion crisis mode, that you can always pull a few
classics from your closet and look sharp—ballet flats, well-fitted
trousers, crisp white button-down shirt, and aviator glasses.

The same is true of pies. It's fun to experiment and express your
culinary creativity with the flavor and contraption du jour. But
when it comes right down to it, most pies—even avant-garde
ones—can trace their roots back to one of a handful of traditional
pies such as apple, pumpkin, and blueberry. Like red lipstick and
the little black dress, these pies never go out of style for a reason:
they have mass appeal. The pies in this chapter are all classics,
but some include a slight flourish to bring them up to date.

Apple Pie

What's more American than apple pie? This humble treat is the quintessential autumnal, American dessert, perfect in its simplicity and frugality. It's wonderful on its own, but in terms of adding a "wow" factor, a scoop of vanilla nondairy ice cream, or even a slice of nondairy Cheddar cheese (as you'll find in some diners), will do the trick. You can also drizzle it with Coconut Dulce de Leche (page 147) and call it Caramel Apple Pie.

Makes one 9-inch (23 cm) pie

1 Basic Double-Crust Pastry
  (page 32) or Gluten-Free
  Double-Crust Pastry (page 33)
5 large, tart apples, peeled and
  chopped
3 tablespoons (23 g) flour,
  (Gluten-free is fine.)
½ cup (100 g) granulated sugar
½ cup (115 g) brown sugar
¼ teaspoon nutmeg
½ teaspoon ground ginger
½ teaspoon cinnamon
¼ teaspoon salt
1 tablespoon (15 ml) vanilla extract
⅔ cup (160 ml) soy half-and-half or
  vanilla soymilk
1 tablespoon (13 g) coarse sugar,
  for sprinkling

Preheat the oven to 425°F (220°C, or gas mark 7).

Divide the dough in half and roll out the top and bottom crusts. Place the bottom crust in the pan and lay the top gently over it to store temporarily. Refrigerate until ready to fill.

Just before baking the pie, in a large bowl, stir together the apples, flour, granulated sugar, brown sugar, spices, salt, vanilla, and half-and-half and spoon into the prepared crust. (Do this just before baking to ensure the crispiest bottom crust possible.) Top with the second crust and crimp the edges as desired. Sprinkle with the coarse sugar.

Place the pie on a foil-lined cookie sheet (to catch any fruit spillover) and bake for 15 minutes. Lower the heat to 350°F (180°C, or gas mark 4) and bake for 45 more minutes, until the top is golden. If the crust seems to brown too quickly, cover the pie with aluminum foil. Allow to cool completely before slicing.

Cherry or Blueberry Pie

Even with all of the exotic pie and tart recipes in this book, good old-fashioned, unadorned cherry pie is my hands-down favorite. Because I am a lazy cook, my version is fuss-free. In other words, I often use frozen fruit, if only because I hate pitting cherries. If you have a cherry tree in your backyard and it's raining down fruit, or if you are the industrious, summa self-reliant type, by all means, pit your cherries. I'm just saying that frozen tastes just about as good as fresh for the same price and less effort.

This pie looks gorgeous with a lattice crust, revealing peek-a-boo squares of red or blue fruit. I also like to make it with a flat top and vent it by making a pattern with my teeny cherry cookie cutter.

Makes one 9-inch (23 cm) pie

5 cups (775 g) pitted fresh or frozen cherries, drained, or 4 cups (580 g) fresh blueberries
1 cup (200 g) sugar
¼ teaspoon salt
3 tablespoons (24 g) cornstarch
½ teaspoon cinnamon
1 Basic Double-Crust Pastry (page 32) or Gluten-Free Double-Crust Pastry (page 34)
1 tablespoon (15 ml) oil, for brushing (optional)
2 teaspoons sugar, for sprinkling (optional)

Preheat the oven to 425°F (220°C, or gas mark 7).

Combine the cherries or blueberries, sugar, salt, cornstarch, and cinnamon in a large bowl. Let it sit for 10 to 15 minutes before pouring it into the crust.

Divide the dough in half and roll out the top and bottom crusts. Pour the filling into the bottom crust. Top with the second crust and vent as desired. If you'd like, brush gently with oil and sprinkle with some coarse or regular sugar.

Place the prepared pie on a foil-lined cookie sheet to catch spillage and save you cleanup time. Bake for 15 minutes and then lower the heat to 350°F (180°C, or gas mark 4) and bake for 35 to 40 minutes or until the top is golden brown. Let cool for at least 2 to 3 hours before slicing.

Peach Pie with Salted Agave Drizzle

Most fruit pies are finished with either a pastry top crust or a crumble topping. But juicy summer peaches are so gloriously orange and happy that it's a shame to cover up their sunny color. So instead, I've topped this classic with a fancy drizzle of agave (punctuated with gorgeous flakes of finishing salt) for modesty—and to complement and balance the flavors. This is divine à la mode, with a scoop of pure vanilla nondairy ice cream.

Makes one 9-inch (23 cm) pie

1 Basic Single-Crust Pastry
  (page 30) or Gluten-Free Single-
  Crust Pastry (page 33)
5 cups (850 g) peeled, 1-inch (2.5 cm)
  chunks ripe peaches (about
  4 or 5 medium peaches)
1 tablespoon (15 ml) lemon juice
½ cup (63 g) all-purpose flour
  (Gluten-free is fine.)
2 teaspoons cornstarch
¾ cup (150 g) granulated sugar
  (add ¼ cup [50 g] more if peaches
  are not sweet)
¼ teaspoon sea salt
½ teaspoon cinnamon
Pinch of ground cloves
Pinch of ground nutmeg

FOR SALTED AGAVE DRIZZLE:
1 cup (320 gl) agave nectar
2 teaspoons large-chunk finishing
  salt, like fleur de sel, Hawaiian,
  black lava, or pink Himalayan
  salt, which looks gorgeous sus-
  pended in the amber liquid

Confectioners' sugar, for dusting

Preheat the oven to 375°F (190°C, or gas mark 5).

Roll out the crust and place in the pan. Crimp the edges and refrigerate, lightly covered, until ready to fill.

Combine the peaches, lemon juice, flour, cornstarch, granulated sugar, salt, and spices in a large bowl. Pour into the crust and bake for 10 minutes. Then lower the heat to 350°F (180°C, or gas mark 4) and bake for 35 to 40 more minutes or until the crust is golden.

Remove from the oven and allow to cool thoroughly at room temperature. Refrigerate for a few hours.

Just before serving, dust with some confectioners' sugar. Slice the pie.

TO MAKE THE AGAVE DRIZZLE: Prepare this just before serving or the salt flakes will melt. In a medium bowl, mix the agave and salt. Pour a bit over the pie slice, allowing some to drip over edge onto the plate. (I recommend a white or light plate to highlight the contrast.) If you want to make just enough for one slice, mix about 1 tablespoon (20 g) agave with about ¼ teaspoon salt. Sprinkle very judiciously with extra salt if you like salt. (I used chocolate sea salt I bought in Portland!)

Gingered-Pear Pie

Pear pie is a basic, use-up-the-harvest pie that I make often from September through November. Adding freshly grated, slightly spicy ginger transforms this pie from classy to sassy. You can crown it with your favorite whipped topping or serve it in a little puddle of Coconut Dulce de Leche (page 147).

Makes one 9-inch (23 cm) pie

---

1 Basic Double-Crust Pastry (page 32) or Gluten-Free Double-Crust Pastry (page 34)

5 ripe pears, peeled and chopped (about 4 cups [680 g])

1 teaspoon lemon, lime, or orange juice (to prevent browning)

¾ cup (150 g) sugar

2 tablespoons (16 g) cornstarch

2 tablespoons (16 g) flour (Gluten-free is fine.)

1-inch (2.5 cm) piece ginger, peeled and grated (about 1 tablespoon [8 g])

½ teaspoon cinnamon

Preheat the oven to 400°F (200°C, or gas mark 6).

Divide the dough in half and roll out the top and bottom crusts. Place the bottom crust in the pan and lay the top gently over it to store temporarily. Refrigerate until ready to fill.

Just before baking the pie, in a large bowl, stir together the pears, juice, sugar, cornstarch, flour, ginger, and cinnamon and spoon into the prepared crust. (Do this just before baking to ensure the crispiest bottom crust possible.) Top with the second crust and crimp the edges as desired.

Place the pie on a foil-lined cookie sheet (to catch any fruit spillover) and bake for 35 to 40 minutes until the top is golden. If the crust seems to brown too quickly, cover the pie with aluminum foil. Allow to cool completely before slicing.

Freeze!

Grating fresh ginger can be tricky. Sometimes you end up with a pile of mush. I discovered, by accident, that if you freeze your ginger first, then grate it, it is much easier. (You can freeze ginger almost indefinitely.)

Retro Strawberry Pie

It was 1978. My frizzy hair was feathered, à la Farrah Fawcett. I was into Led Zeppelin and Monty Python, and I was in love. My first boyfriend was my best friend for a year. We played guitar and vowed to be the next Lennon and McCartney songwriting team. His grandma made this pie for us, and every time I taste it, the jammy sweetness transports me back to that innocent summer. This pie is magically light—just like a first love. It's the perfect dessert during the hot summer months, when strawberries are sweetest, or after a heavy dinner. Oh, and it works for Valentine's Day, too.

Makes one 9-inch (23 cm) pie

1 All-Purpose Cookie Crust made with vanilla cookies or animal crackers (page 35)

3 tablespoons (24 g) cornstarch

6 tablespoons (90 ml) water

2 quarts (1160 g) strawberries, hulled and cut in half (reserve 12 of the prettiest, plumpest specimens for the bottom of the pie)

1 cup (200 g) sugar

¼ teaspoon salt

1 tablespoon (3 g) agar flakes

1 recipe Whipped Nut Topping made with cashews (page 144) or Coconut Whipped Topping (page 146) or store-bought nondairy whipped cream or nondairy, non-hydrogenated whipped topping

Leftover Makeover

Do you have strawberry mash left over? Pour it into ramekins to make individual-size fruit puddings. Or save it to use in smoothies or over ice cream.

Preheat the oven to 350°F (180°C, or gas mark 4).

Blind bake the cookie crust for 10 minutes (use pie weights).

In a small bowl, mix the cornstarch and water with a fork or small whisk until smooth. Set aside.

Arrange the 12 prettiest raw strawberries cut-side down on the crust. Set aside.

Quarter the remaining strawberries and use a potato masher to mash in a medium bowl.

In a medium saucepan over high heat, bring the sugar, salt, and mashed strawberries to a rolling boil, stirring occasionally. When boiling, add the agar, lower the heat, and simmer for about 1 minute. Whisk in the cornstarch mixture. Be careful because the mixture bubbles up. Whisking occasionally, cook until very thick and glossy, about 10 minutes. Remove from the heat and let cool for about 5 minutes.

Carefully spoon the cooked, slightly cooled mashed berries over the top of the fresh strawberries. Do not overfill! Let it sit on the counter until cool enough to handle, about an hour, and then cover tightly with plastic and refrigerate overnight. Slice with a very sharp knife and a pie server. Serve cold with your favorite whipped topping.

Note

To make this pie gluten-free, simply make your cookie crust using gluten-free cookies.

Strawberry-Rhubarb Pie

Spotting a bin of magenta-green rhubarb stalks in the market is the first sign for me that spring is coming, even before primroses, robins, and the groundhog's predictions. Rhubarb and strawberries are a classic pairing. Not only do their red hues complement each other, but the sweetness of the berries also seems to temper the slight acidic bite of the rhubarb. Topping this with a crumble makes this a breakfast no-brainer, delicious with a cup of Earl Grey tea.

Makes one 9-inch (23 cm) pie

1 Basic Single-Crust Pastry (page 30) or Gluten-Free Single-Crust Pastry (page 33)

FOR CRUMBLE TOPPING:
¾ cup (170 g) packed brown sugar
3 tablespoons (23 g) flour (Gluten-free is fine.)
3 tablespoons (18 g) rolled oats (Gluten-free is fine.)
4 tablespoons (56 g) margarine, cubed
1 teaspoon cinnamon
¼ teaspoon nutmeg
¼ teaspoon salt

FOR FILLING:
¾ cup (150 g) granulated sugar
¼ cup (31 g) flour (Gluten-free is fine.)
1 tablespoon (8 g) cornstarch
¼ teaspoon baking soda
¼ teaspoon cinnamon
¼ teaspoon ground ginger
4 cups (488 g) ½-inch pieces rhubarb
2 cups (340 g) quartered strawberries

Preheat the oven to 375°F (190°C, or gas mark 5).

Roll out the dough and place in a greased pie pan. Flute the edges as desired. Refrigerate until the filling is ready.

TO MAKE THE TOPPING: In a large bowl, combine the topping ingredients with a fork. It's supposed to be clumpy, so don't get too fussy when mixing.

TO MAKE THE FILLING: In another large bowl, mix the filling ingredients.

Pour the filling into the pie crust. Scatter the crumble topping over the filling. Cover the pie edges lightly with foil or a pie guard to prevent browning. Bake for 20 minutes then remove the foil, and bake for 25 to 30 more minutes, or until the crumble is golden brown. Allow to cool completely in the refrigerator for at least 2 hours before serving.

Shoo-Fly Pie

This is a regional Pennsylvania pie, popularized by the Amish who live in rural Lancaster and sell them to "English" (a.k.a. non-Amish) tourists. It's quite starchy and is made from humble ingredients, so if you know this recipe, you can put together a dessert pie no matter how bare your cupboard is. Nothing is more comforting than a slice of this carby heaven with a nice cold glass of soymilk. And it's shamefully easy to make.

How did this pie get such a silly name? It's quite sweet, so when the Amish ladies set these sticky pies on the windowsill to cool, they constantly had to "shoo" away the flies that were drawn to the sugar.

Makes one 9-inch (23 cm) pie

----

1 Basic Single-Crust Pastry
(page 30)

FOR BOTTOM LAYER:
1 cup (340 g) molasses
¾ cup (175 ml) hot water
1 teaspoon baking soda

FOR TOP LAYER:
1½ cups (188 g) flour
1 cup (225 g) packed brown sugar
¼ teaspoon salt
4 tablespoons (50 g) vegetable
shortening
1 teaspoon vanilla extract

Preheat the oven to 400°F (200°C, or gas mark 6).

Roll out the dough and place in a greased pie pan. Flute the edges as desired. Refrigerate until the filling is ready.

TO MAKE THE BOTTOM LAYER: In a medium bowl, mix the molasses, hot water, and baking soda. Don't be alarmed when it starts to foam and resemble a science experiment. This is normal. Place the pie pan on a cookie sheet (in case of spillover). Pour about three-fourths of the mixture into the pie shell.

TO MAKE THE TOP LAYER: In a large bowl, mix the flour, brown sugar, and salt, then add the shortening and vanilla, and cut with a pastry cutter into coarse crumbs. Scatter atop molasses layer, and then drizzle the remaining one-fourth of the molasses mixture over the top.

Bake for 15 minutes, and then lower the temperature to 350°F (180°C, or gas mark 4). Bake for 30 minutes longer; the topping should just start to turn golden. Cool for at least 2 hours before cutting.

Nectarine-Raspberry Pie

This is an unusual pie only in that these fruits are generally reserved fresh for tarts. But I contend that you can make a pie out of anything. The sweetness of summer's juiciest nectarines, with a refreshingly acerbic raspberry counterpoint, naturally begs to be encased in a robe of flaky pie crust. Try this one à la mode.

Makes one 9-inch (23 cm) pie

1 Basic Double-Crust Pastry (page 32) or Gluten-Free Double-Crust Pastry (page 34)
4 cups (680 g) peeled, 1-inch (2.5 cm) chunks ripe nectarines (about 5 medium)
1 cup (125 g) raspberries
1 tablespoon (15 ml) lemon or lime juice
2 tablespoons (16 g) flour (Gluten-free is fine.)
2 tablespoons (16 g) cornstarch
½ cup (100 g) sugar (add ¼ cup [50 g] more if fruit is not sweet)
½ teaspoon cinnamon
¼ teaspoon powdered ginger
¼ teaspoon sea salt
2 tablespoons (28 ml) nondairy creamer, for brushing crust
1 teaspoon coarse sugar, for sprinkling
Confectioners' sugar, for dusting

Preheat the oven to 400°F (200°C, or gas mark 6).

Roll out the bottom crust and place in a pan. Roll out the top crust and set aside. Refrigerate, lightly covered, until ready to fill.

Gently toss the nectarines, raspberries, lemon juice, flour, cornstarch, sugar, spices, and salt in a large bowl. Pour into the bottom crust. Cut desired slits into the top crust (or use a pie bird). Cover the filling with the top crust, crimp the edges, brush with creamer, and then sprinkle with sugar. Place on a cookie sheet (in case of spillover).

Bake for 15 minutes, and then lower the heat to 350°F (180°C, or gas mark 4) and bake for 50 to 60 more minutes or until the crust is golden.

Remove from the oven and allow to cool thoroughly at room temperature. Dust with confectioners' sugar before serving.

Crumble-Top Berry Pie

I love the straightforward sweetness of a mixed berry pie. With oodles of juicy berries spilling out as you slice it, this pie is a messy affair—I like to think of it as a reconstructed fruit crisp. But the best-tasting foods seem to be the messiest ones.

Each pie you make using this recipe will be unique because the berries' various flavors and subtleties come out during baking. This is such a versatile recipe because you can mix and match berries to your heart, pantry, or wallet's content. It's a great way to use up a summer harvest or a stash of frozen berries during the colder months. This tastes scrumptious with a dollop of Coconut Whipped Topping (page 146) or nondairy ice cream. If you're serving this to your guests, a drizzle of Chocolate Sauce (page 149) can take this pie from humble to haughty.

Makes one 9-inch (23 cm) pie

1 Basic Single-Crust Pastry (page 30) or Gluten-Free Single-Crust Pastry (page 33)

FOR CRUMBLE:
¼ cup (20 g) oats (Gluten-free is fine.)
½ cup (60 g) flour (Gluten-free is fine.)
¼ cup (40 g) chopped nuts
1 teaspoon cinnamon
½ cup (115 g) packed brown sugar
¼ teaspoon salt
6 tablespoons (84 g) margarine

FOR BERRY FILLING:
5 cups (about 725 g) your favorite fresh or frozen berries (e.g., rasp-berries, blackberries, blueberries, strawberries; if using frozen, do not thaw first)
¾ cup (150 g) granulated sugar
1 teaspoon lemon juice
¼ cup (30 g) flour (Gluten-free is fine.)
3 tablespoons (24 g) cornstarch
Zest of 1 orange, lemon, or lime (about 1 teaspoon)

Preheat the oven to 375°F (190°C, or gas mark 5).

Roll out the dough and place in a pie pan. Refrigerate until ready to fill.

TO MAKE THE CRUMBLE: Combine the oats, flour, nuts, cinnamon, brown sugar, and salt in a large bowl. Dice the margarine and toss with the other ingredients. Use your fingers to massage the margarine into the flour mixture. Do not overmix.

TO MAKE THE FILLING: Mix the filling ingredients in a large bowl.

Pour the berry mixture into the pie crust, and then top with the crumble. Place the pan on a cookie sheet and bake for 40 minutes or until the topping is golden. Allow to cool completely before serving.

Crumble Jumble

You can use this crumble topping to replace the pastry topping for virtually any fruit pie in this book. Like-wise, you can make this pie crustless and call it Berry Crumble.

Pumpkin Pie

This is a variation of one of the first vegan pie recipes I developed. I came up with this little number in my early twenties, when I first seriously delved into pie baking. It became my "practical joke" pie. Guests would taste it, proclaim their love for it, and beg me for the recipe. Then I would casually drop the T-bomb—and tell them there was tofu in it. The typical reaction was "Whaaaaaat?" And this was twenty years ago, so if you think tofu is misunderstood now, just imagine its reputation back then. Bottom line is, besides being a holiday and cold-month classic, this pie is a great intro-to-tofu for skeptics. It demonstrates that tofu, like other bland ingredients (e.g., flour, milks), takes on whatever flavors you infuse it with. To add an element of surprise, make this pie using a nontraditional nut or cookie crust.

To make this gluten-free, use the Gluten-Free Single-Crust Pastry (page 33), Nutty Crust (page 36), or All-Purpose Cookie Crust made with gluten-free cookies (page 35).

Makes one 9-inch (23 cm) pie

1 Basic Single-Crust Pastry (page 30), Gluten-free Single Crust Pastry (page 33), Nutty Crust (page 36), or All-Purpose Cookie Crust (page 35)

1 can (15-ounces, or 425 g) unsweetened pumpkin

24 ounces (680 g) aseptic-packaged tofu (Do not use refrigerated tofu; it is too grainy for this recipe.)

½ cup (100 g) granulated sugar

¼ cup (60 g) packed brown sugar

¼ teaspoon salt

1½ teaspoons cinnamon

1 teaspoon powdered ginger

¼ teaspoon ground cloves

¼ teaspoon nutmeg

1 heaping tablespoon (8 g) soy flour

4 tablespoons (60 ml) water

Preheat the oven to 425°F (220°C, or gas mark 7).

Roll out the dough and place in a greased pie pan. Flute the edges as desired. Or if using a nut or cookie crust, prepare the crust and press into the pan. Refrigerate until the filling is ready.

Blend all of the remaining ingredients in a food processor or in a blender until well incorporated. Better to err on the side of caution and overprocess rather than underprocess.

Pour the filling into the crust, leaving ¼ inch (6 mm) of space to the crust edge, and mound it slightly in the center. Bake for 15 minutes and then lower the heat to 350°F (180°C, or gas mark 4) and bake for 35 minutes or until the pie top is golden. Refrigerate for at least 4 hours before slicing.

Orange You Glad You Have Leftover Filling?

I love bad puns. And I love mini crustless pumpkin pies. Depending on the kind of crust you have, you may have leftover filling. To make crustless pies, pour the filling into individual ramekins and bake at 350°F (180°C, or gas mark 4) for 15 to 20 minutes. Or use unbaked filling in smoothies.

Sweet Potato Pie

Y'all need to try this. This pie is a classic that hails from the American South—soul food that feeds your body and soul and screams comfort. You can substitute margarine for the coconut oil, but only in emergencies, please! The rich, nutty coconut essence is a gorgeous, silky backdrop to the creamy sweet potato, and your taste buds will thank you. Never one to leave well enough alone, I like to top this pie with a healthy dollop of Whipped Nut Topping made with cashews (page 144) or Coconut Whipped Topping (page 146). Or a scoop of vanilla nondairy ice cream. Or both!

Makes one 9-inch (23 cm) pie

To make this gluten-free, use the Gluten-Free Single-Crust Pastry (page 33), Nutty Crust (page 36), or All-Purpose Cookie Crust made with gluten-free cookies (page 35).

1 Basic Single-Crust Pastry (page 30), Gluten-free Single Crust Pastry (page 33), Nutty Crust (page 36), or All-Purpose Cookie Crust (page 35)

2¼ cups (506 g) cooked sweet potatoes (well drained, if boiled)

¾ cup (170 g) packed brown sugar

¾ teaspoon cinnamon

½ teaspoon powdered ginger

¼ teaspoon garam masala

¼ teaspoon salt

¼ cup (60 ml) coconut oil, melted, or margarine

1 teaspoon vanilla extract

1 tablespoon (15 ml) rum (optional)

¾ cup (175 ml) nondairy milk

⅓ cup (33 g) pecan halves

Preheat the oven to 375°F (190°C, or gas mark 5).

Roll out the dough and place in a greased pie pan. Flute the edges as desired. Or if using a nut or cookie crust, prepare the crust and press into the pan. Refrigerate until the filling is ready.

Blend the sweet potatoes, brown sugar, spices, salt, oil, vanilla, and rum in a food processor or in a blender until well incorporated. Add the milk a little at a time and blend until the filling is smooth.

Pour the filling into the crust, leaving ¼ inch (6 mm) of space to the crust edge. Decorate with the pecan halves. Bake for 15 minutes, and then lower the heat to 325°F (170°C, or gas mark 3) and bake for 50 to 60 minutes until the top is golden and slightly cracked, a cake tester comes out clean, and the pie is no longer wobbly. (If using a pastry crust, be sure to check after about 40 minutes and add a crust guard if the edges are browning too quickly.) Refrigerate the pie for at least 4 hours before slicing.

Surprisingly Sweet Parsnip Pie

Let's get to the root of the matter—*groan*!—root veggies are not just for savory foods. Although we are comfortable using orange vegetables like carrots and sweet potatoes in desserts, other tubers also make wonderful, sweet bases. The parsnip is inherently sweet with an undertone of heat that reminds me of ginger. Try this unconventional autumnal pie. You will be pleasantly surprised, especially if you're already a parsnip fan. Use gluten-free gingersnaps for a gluten-free pie.

Makes one 9-inch (23 cm) pie

1 All-Purpose Cookie Crust made with gingersnaps (page 35)
2 pounds (900 g) parsnips, peeled and cut into 1-inch (2.5 cm) chunks (about 4 cups [440 g])
1 box (12 ounces, or 336 g) aseptic-packaged tofu (Do not use refrigerated tofu; it is too grainy for this recipe.)
½ teaspoon salt
¾ cup (170 g) packed light brown sugar
1 teaspoon cinnamon
½ teaspoon ground ginger
¼ teaspoon nutmeg
1 teaspoon vanilla extract
Nondairy whipped topping (optional)

Preheat the oven to 425°F (220°C, or gas mark 7).

Prepare the cookie crust and press into a pan. Refrigerate until the filling is ready.

Boil the parsnips until soft, about 15 minutes. Place in a large bowl and mash until creamy.

Blend the remaining ingredients in a food processor or in a blender until well incorporated then add the parsnips and process until smooth-ish and well combined. You'll need to scrape down the and processor every now and then.

Pour the filling into the crust, leaving ¼ inch (6 mm) of space to the crust edge. Bake for 15 minutes and then lower the heat to 350°F (180°C, or gas mark 4) and bake for 30 to 35 minutes until the pie top is golden. Refrigerate for at least 4 hours before slicing.

Petite Parsnip Puddings

Have you got leftover filling? Pour into ramekin dishes and bake at 350°F (180°C, or gas mark 4) for about 15 to 20 minutes or until firm.

Mini Linzertortes

The famous linzertorte hails from, you guessed it, Linz, Austria, and it's quite popular at Christmas. It is basically just a slightly fancier version of the Crostata di Marmellata (opposite page), which means that it's easy to make despite its air of ruby-red sophistication. The linzertorte is usually made as a standard 9-inch (23 cm) torte. But downsized to single-serving tortes, they don't look quite as snobbish as the full-size version. If you want to make the full size, by all means do. (You may need to bake it an additional 10 minutes or so.)

Makes four 4-inch (10 cm) tortes

½ cup (73 g) toasted almonds
1½ cups (188 g) flour, plus up to
    ¼ cup (31 g) extra, if needed
½ cup (115 g) packed brown sugar
¾ cup (175 ml) nondairy milk
½ cup (112 g) margarine
1 teaspoon baking soda
¼ teaspoon salt
½ teaspoon cinnamon
¼ teaspoon nutmeg
1 teaspoon lemon zest
1 heaping cup (320 g) raspberry jam

Preheat the oven to 400°F (200°C, or gas mark 6).

Process the nuts into a fine powder in the food processor, and then add the remaining ingredients except the jam. Transfer to a large bowl, and using your hands, form a dough ball. If it's too sticky, add more flour, 1 tablespoon (8 g) at a time, until it's easy to handle.

Remove one-third of the dough ball and set aside. Roll out the larger dough ball to fit your pans. The dough will be a bit crumbly, but this is normal. Place into your pans and press down to even out the appearance.

Spoon the raspberry filling into the crusts. Roll out the remaining dough and either use cookie cutters to cut out small shapes or use a pastry wheel to cut strips for a lattice-style top crust. Place the desired crust atop the jam. Bake for 25 to 30 minutes until the jam is bubbly and the crust is golden brown. Dust with confectioners' sugar when cool.

Variations
- Add 1 tablespoon (5 g) cocoa powder to the crust.
- Substitute hazelnuts or walnuts for the almonds.
- Substitute lingonberry, apricot, or fig jam for the raspberry.

How to Toast Nuts

Preheat the oven to 400°F (200°C, or gas mark 6). Spread the nuts on a cookie sheet and toast for 8 to 10 minutes or until just slightly browned. Chances are, your nose will know when they're done before your kitchen timer goes off.

 # Crostata di Marmellata

This is hands-down the easiest recipe in this book. Your favorite fruit jam sandwiched between two layers of flaky pastry, decorated with a simple lattice top—think of it as a fancy Italian Pop-Tart. This is a go-to for a fast breakfast or when you have surprise guests coming over for dinner and you need to make a quick but impressive dessert. A dollop of Coconut Whipped Topping (page 146) or nondairy ice cream takes this over the top. It's a good one for the kiddos to help out with, too.

You will only need one and a half of the double-crust recipe because you will leave more of the top open than with a traditional lattice-crust top. Freeze the rest for another use or use the remainder to make Happy Little Scrappies (page 34). Good options for the jam include strawberry, blackberry, *frutti di bosco* (fruits of the forest), fig, apricot, or orange marmalade.

- -

Makes one 9-inch (23 cm) tart

- -

1 Basic Double-Crust Pastry (page 32) or Gluten-Free Double-Crust Pastry (page 34)
1 jar (12 ounces, or 336 g) of your favorite jam or marmalade

TartSmart: **Quiche**

Crostata (plural: crostate) is Italian for "tart." *Delizioso* is Italian for yum!

Preheat the oven to 375°F (190°C, or gas mark 5).

Roll out the bottom crust and place in the pan. Spread the jam on top. Roll out the top crust (half of the remaining dough) and make ½-inch (1.3 cm) strips. Using a pastry cutter makes them look neater, but you can also cut them with a knife or roll them for a more authentic "nonna" look. Carefully place atop the jam and weave as shown on page 128. Place on a cookie sheet (to catch any spillage) and bake for 35 to 40 minutes or until the crust is golden brown.

* Chapter 4 *

Decadent and Creamy Pies

MANY PIES—LIKE MOST FRUIT PIES AND RAW
PIES—are inherently vegan. But creamy and traditional decadent
pie fillings tend to lean heavily on full-fat dairy products. Fear not,
my herbivore friends. You can have your pie and eat it, too. These
scrumptious little numbers are just as orgasmically rich as dairy-
based pies, but they have a few special bonuses: they are cruelty-
free, cholesterol-free, and hormone-free.

Banana Cream Pie

Many people associate humble banana cream pie with trashy American diners, but really, this simple pie deserves to rise above its low-brow reputation. Banana cream pie is my go-to comfort dessert. I'd take a serving of this silky slice of heaven over chocolate anything, any day. And because this vegan version doesn't contain artery-clogging creams, it borders on healthy. Kinda, sorta.

When it comes to banana cream pies, there are as many versions as there are cooks. People argue over which crust to use (Pastry? Nut crust? Graham cracker crust?) and over the proportions and toppings (Pudding? Whipped cream? Cooked sauce?). I am of the vanilla-cookie-crust banana-pudding whipped-topping ilk. This combination gives me the maximum amount of creamy comfort for the minimum amount of effort. But feel free to substitute your favorites if you must. Use gluten-free cookies for a gluten-free pie.

Makes one 9-inch (23 cm) pie

---

1 All-Purpose Cookie Crust made with graham crackers, animal crackers, or vanilla or chocolate cookies (page 35)

FOR PUDDING:
2 cups (475 ml) nondairy milk
½ cup (112 g) brown or (100 g) granulated sugar
¼ teaspoon salt
1 teaspoon vanilla extract
Scrapings from 1 vanilla bean
¼ cup (32 g) cornstarch
1 teaspoon agar flakes

FOR BANANA LAYER:
4 or 5 medium ripe bananas
1½ tablespoons (23 ml) freshly squeezed lemon juice (to prevent browning)

2 recipes Coconut Whipped Topping (page 146)
1 or 2 bananas, for garnish

Press the crust into a pie pan.

TO MAKE THE PUDDING: In a medium saucepan, combine the milk, sugar, salt, vanilla, and bean scrapings (if using) and bring to a boil. Whisk in the cornstarch, about 1 tablespoon (8 g) at a time, stirring well to avoid "clumpage." Add the agar flakes. Decrease the heat to low and cook, whisking constantly, until it thickens, about 10 minutes. Remove from heat. When at room temperature, cover and refrigerate for at least 2 hours. (You can do this step the night before if you are pressed for time.)

TO MAKE THE BANANA LAYER: Just before assembling the pie, slice the bananas about ¼- to ½-inch (6 to 13 mm) thick and toss with the lemon juice to prevent browning. Layer the bananas in the bottom of your cookie crust. Top with the pudding and then gently top with the Coconut Whipped Topping. Chill for at least 2 hours before serving and then garnish with freshly sliced bananas upon serving.

Creamy Chocolate Tart

This is a ginormous, in-your-face, no-holds-barred chocolate pudding pie for serious chocoholics only, not for the faint of heart or the calorie conscious. I like to brighten the earthiness of the cocoa mass (and I do mean mass!) with some orange zest and a shot of Cointreau, my favorite orange-based liqueur. A thin slice is the perfect ending to a light meal. And don't skimp on ingredients: the better the chocolate, the better the pie. If you're going to splurge, you may as well make it worth your while, right? Use gluten-free cookies for a gluten-free pie.

Makes one 11-inch (28 cm) tart

FOR CRUST:

2 cups (144 g) chocolate cookie
    crumbs (about 4 cups [144 g]
    cookies, give or take)
1 teaspoon vanilla extract
5 tablespoons (70 g) margarine
¼ teaspoon salt

FOR FILLING:

1 cup (235 ml) plus 2 tablespoons
    (28 ml) soy creamer or coconut
    milk, divided
1½ cups (263 g) best-quality nondairy
    dark chocolate chips or buttons
1 tablespoon (8 g) cornstarch
2 teaspoons orange zest
1 tablespoon (14 g) margarine
1 tablespoon (15 ml) Cointreau,
    brandy, or rum (in order of prefer-
    ence; optional, but wonderful)
Pinch of salt

Garnishes, as desired (see sidebar)

Preheat the oven to 400°F (200°C, or gas mark 6).

TO MAKE THE CRUST: Combine all the crust ingredients in a large bowl and press into an 11-inch (28 cm) tart pan. Bake for 8 to 10 minutes. Let cool before filling.

TO MAKE THE FILLING: In a medium saucepan over medium heat, bring 1 cup (235 ml) of the milk to a boil. Add the chocolate, decrease the heat to low, and cook, stirring now and then, until it's melted. In a small bowl, make a slurry with the cornstarch and remaining 2 tablespoons (28 ml) milk. Once smooth, whisk into the chocolate, along with the zest, margarine, Cointreau, and salt and cook over low heat until thick, whisking often, about 5 minutes. Immediately pour into the cooled crust. Refrigerate for 2 hours before serving.

Variations

- Skip the crust, just make the filling, and call it Death by Chocolate Pudding.
- To temper the chocolate hit, spread 1 cup (320 g) raspberry or apricot jam or orange marmalade over the bottom of the cooled, cooked cookie crust before adding the chocolate.
- Conversely, to raise the hedonism quotient, spread 1 cup (260 g) chocolate-hazelnut spread or peanut butter over the cooled crust before adding the chocolate mixture. You can use a knife to swirl the latter and make a pretty marble pattern.

Talking Garnish

Try one of these garnishes.
- Fresh raspberries or sliced strawberries
- Sliced orange rind   • Candied orange rind
- Shaved chocolate   • Nuts
- Confectioners' sugar, sifted over a stencil

Chocolate-Peanut Butter Pie

Some people have a sweet tooth. I also have a fat tooth, so this pie satisfies both my vices in a single serving. This is a decadent one-two punch!

Chocolate and peanut butter have a natural affinity—they bring out the best in each other—and not surprisingly, just about everyone loves the combination. This pie is truly rich, so serve just a sliver to your guests, along with a cup of joe. Use gluten-free cookies for a gluten-free pie.

Makes one 9-inch (23 cm) pie

----

1 All-Purpose Cookie Crust made with chocolate cookies (page 35)

FOR PEANUT BUTTER MOUSSE:
½ cup (130 g) peanut butter
½ cup (115 g) nondairy cream cheese
¾ cup (90 g) confectioners' sugar
¼ teaspoon salt (Skip if peanut butter is salted.)

FOR CHOCOLATE–PEANUT BUTTER MOUSSE:
½ cup (130 g) chocolate peanut butter (I love Peanut Butter and Company's Dark Chocolate Dreams.)
½ cup (115 g) nondairy cream cheese
½ cup (60 g) confectioners' sugar
¼ teaspoon salt (Skip if peanut butter is salted.)

Preheat the oven to 400°F (200°C, or gas mark 6).

Press the crust into a pan. Bake for 10 minutes and then cool completely before filling.

TO MAKE THE PEANUT BUTTER MOUSSE: Mix all the ingredients in a bowl with a spatula until combined. Spread on the bottom of the cooled crust.

TO MAKE THE CHOCOLATE–PEANUT BUTTER MOUSSE: Mix all the ingredients in a bowl with a spatula until combined. Gently spread atop the peanut butter layer. Chill for at least 2 hours before serving. I like to freeze for an hour before slicing.

S'more Pie

Traditional s'mores are made over the campfire with just three basic ingredients: graham crackers, marshmallow, and chocolate. But marshmallow is traditionally made with gelatin, which, if you didn't know, is made from cows' hooves (ew!), a fact that may skeeve out even the staunchest of omnivores. This vegan version uses Ricemellow Creme, a vegan marshmallow fluff made with brown rice syrup. No campfire or cows' hooves required. Use gluten-free graham crackers for a gluten-free pie.

Makes one 9-inch (23 cm) pie

1 All-Purpose Cookie Crust made
  with graham crackers (page 35)

FOR CHOCOLATE MOUSSE:
1 cup (175 g) nondairy dark or
  semisweet chocolate chips
½ cup (60 g) confectioners' sugar
1 box (12 ounces, or 336 g) aseptic-
  packaged soft tofu (Do not use
  refrigerated tofu; it is too grainy
  for this recipe.)
⅛ teaspoon salt
1 tablespoon (15 ml) rum or brandy,
  or 2 teaspoons vanilla or banana
  extract

1 container (10 ounces, or 280 g)
  Ricemellow Creme
½ cup (88 g) nondairy dark chocolate chips, vegan chocolate
  sprinkles, or chocolate shavings,
  for garnish

Press the graham cracker crust into a pan.

TO MAKE THE CHOCOLATE MOUSSE: Melt the chocolate chips in a microwave-safe bowl in the microwave at 50 percent power, about 3 to 5 minutes, depending on the voltage of your microwave. (Stop about halfway through and stir.) Blend the melted chocolate in a food processor along with the sugar, tofu, and salt. Process until smooth and creamy. Err on the side of overprocessing—you are aiming for creamy, not clumpy. Add the booze.

Spread the mousse or extract evenly in the graham cracker crust, and then top with the Ricemellow Creme, spreading gently with an offset spatula. Scatter the chocolate chips on top. Chill for at least 2 hours before serving.

Fluffernutter Pie

As a kid, you knew it was going to be a good day when you dipped into your lunch box and found a Fluffernutter sandwich waiting for you along with your requisite apple and carrot sticks. Peanut butter and marshmallow for lunch is about as American as it gets. Until now, when we are having the Fluffernutter for dessert. I added a chocolate cookie crust for an extra hit of decadence. You can use either creamy or chunky peanut butter—creamy looks nicer but chunky tastes better. Sometimes, I make a double batch of the filling and either eat it as pudding or use it to make decadent frozen pops. For the crust, you may substitute graham crackers, animal crackers, or vanilla cookies, or any gluten-free cookie or cracker.

Makes one 9-inch (23 cm) pie

1 All-Purpose Cookie Crust made
  with chocolate cookies (page 35)
½ cup (130 g) peanut butter
¼ cup (60 g) nondairy cream cheese
½ teaspoon vanilla extract
1 cup plus 2 tablespoons (135 g)
  confectioners' sugar
¼ teaspoon salt
1 to 1½ cups (96 to 144 g) vegan
  marshmallow fluff (I use
  Ricemellow Creme.)
A few peanuts, for garnish

Preheat the oven to 400°F (200°C, or gas mark 6).

Press the crust into a pan and bake for 8 to 10 minutes or until firm. Let cool completely before filling.

In a food processor, cream together the peanut butter, cream cheese, vanilla, sugar, and salt until completely smooth. It is better to over-process than underprocess.

Spread the filling in the cooled crust. Refrigerate for at least 2 hours. Just before serving, top with the marshmallow fluff and garnish with a few peanuts.

Variations

An astonishing variety of gourmet peanut butters now grace the super-market shelves. I love the ones made by Peanut Butter and Company, but many other brands are also available. Mix and match with appropriate cookie crusts to create unique combinations. Here are some ideas:

* Vegan chocolate hazelnut spread (you'll probably want to cut back on the sugar) with chocolate cookie crust
* Cinnamon raisin peanut butter with graham cracker crust
* Chocolate peanut butter with vanilla cookie crust
* Maple peanut butter with vanilla cookie crust

Frozen Spumoni Pie

This frozen pie is a feast for the palate and the eyes, thanks to its contrasting layers of flavor and color. Think spumoni in a pie. The thing I love most about this pie is that you get a huge wow factor for very little effort. The only culinary skill required for this pie, aside from knowing how to operate a food processor for the cookie crust, is the ability to transfer softened ice cream from container to pie shell. For this reason, it's a great recipe for kids. Use gluten-free cookies or graham crackers for a gluten-free pie.

Makes one 9-inch (23 cm) pie

1 **All-Purpose Cookie Crust made with graham crackers or chocolate or vanilla cookies (page 35)**
1 **cup (140 g) each of vanilla, chocolate, and strawberry nondairy ice cream, softened at room temperature for ½ hour before using**
1 **cup (175 g) nondairy chocolate chips**
1 **cup (170 g) sliced strawberries**
1 **cup (64 g) vegan chocolate sprinkles**

Press the cookie crust into a pie pan. Spread the softened chocolate ice cream on the crust. Cover and freeze for 2 hours or until hardened. Repeat with the vanilla ice cream and when that layer is frozen, follow with the strawberry ice cream. Let the pie sit at room temperature for about 15 minutes before serving. Adorn each slice with a serving of each desired topping and serve.

Variation

Instead of this spumoni version, try mixing and matching other favorite ice cream flavors. Choose flavors that are compatible and, ideally, colors that contrast, such as peanut butter and chocolate fudge or coffee and vanilla.

Frozen Chocolate Mudslide Pie

As you probably have guessed from the name, this is serious chocoholic fodder —only for die-hard chocolate fans. I find myself reaching for this recipe after a particularly trying day or whenever I host a dinner party because it's so easy to prepare. Chocolate overload. And easy. What's not to love? Use gluten-free cookies for a gluten-free pie.

Makes one 9-inch (23 cm) pie

----

1 All-Purpose Cookie Crust made with chocolate cookies (page 35)

2 tablespoons (10 g) Dutch cocoa powder, divided

3 cups (420 g) chocolate or fudge-centric nondairy ice cream (or a combination), softened at room temperature for ½ hour before using

½ cup (88 g) nondairy dark chocolate chips

½ cup (72 g) of your favorite chopped nuts

½ cup (120 ml) chocolate sauce, store-bought or homemade (page 149)

Optional decorations for finished pie (e.g., mint leaves, nondairy chocolate chips, nuts, chocolate shavings, chocolate sprinkles)

Press the cookie crust into a pie pan. Sprinkle the bottom of the crust with 1 tablespoon (5 g) of the cocoa.

In a large bowl, mix the softened ice cream with the remaining 1 tablespoon (5 g) cocoa powder. Spread on the crust (and if there's any left over, have a dish as a chef's reward). Top with the chocolate chips and nuts. Cover and freeze for 2 hours or until hardened.

Drizzle the chocolate sauce on top, Jackson Pollock-style, and freeze for another ½ hour or longer. Decorate the top (or not), slice, and serve.

Frozen Grasshopper Pie

This pie gets its inspiration from the famous Girl Scout Thin Mint Cookie. It's very refreshing—perfect to clear your palate after a sticky summer picnic or barbecue. You feel cooler just looking at it. Use gluten-free cookies for a gluten-free pie.

Makes one 9-inch (23 cm) pie

------

1 All-Purpose Cookie Crust made with chocolate cookies (page 35)

1 pint (280 g) each of mint chocolate chip and chocolate nondairy ice cream, softened at room temperature for ½ hour before using (see Note)

2 tablespoons (28 ml) crème de menthe liqueur

½ cup (120 ml) chocolate sauce, store-bought or homemade (page 149), optional

Press the cookie crust into a pie pan. Spread softened chocolate ice cream on the crust (and if there's any left over, have a dish as a chef's reward). Cover and freeze for 2 hours or until hardened.

In a large bowl, mix the softened mint ice cream with the crème de menthe, for an extra shot of flavor. Add natural color (see Note) if using. Spread atop the frozen mint ice cream mixture, and cover and freeze for 2 more hours, or until hardened. Slice and serve drizzled with the chocolate sauce, if desired.

Note

If you are buying all-natural nondairy ice cream, chances are it won't be the fluorescent green color we've come to associate with mint chocolate chip. Fear not. Make your own natural green coloring by adding ¼ to ⅛ teaspoon or so of chlorella or spirulina powder to the softened ice cream. The color will be more pastel than neon.

Butterscotch Pudding Pie

Food has gotten so pretentious over the past five years, and what I love most about this pie is its down-homey-ness. There's no frills, just salty-buttery goodness. You can also skip the crust and just make the pudding! Jazz it up with nuts, chocolate chips, or a drizzle of the darker Butterscotch Sauce (page 148), which contrasts nicely against the blond filling.

Makes one 9-inch (23 cm) pie

1 Basic Single-Crust Pastry (page 30) or Gluten-Free Single-Crust Pastry (page 33)
1 cup (235 ml) nondairy milk, divided
3 tablespoons (24 g) cornstarch
1 cup (225 g) packed brown sugar
1 cup (230 g) nondairy sour cream
¼ teaspoon salt
1 tablespoon (14 g) margarine
1 teaspoon vanilla extract
Nuts, nondairy chocolate chips, or sprinkling sugar, for decorating (optional)

Preheat the oven to 400°F (200°C, or gas mark 6).

Roll out the crust and fit in the pan. Line with foil, add pie weights, and bake for about 30 minutes or until the crust is golden. Allow to cool completely before filling.

In a small bowl, make a slurry by whisking together ¼ cup (60 ml) of the milk and the cornstarch until absolutely smooth. Set aside.

In a small saucepan over medium heat, whisk together the remaining ¾ cup (175 ml) milk, brown sugar, sour cream, and salt. Bring to a gentle boil, stirring occasionally. Keep a close watch over the pot so it doesn't boil over! Lower the heat and whisk in the slurry. Cook over low heat, whisking occasionally, until very thick, about 10 minutes. Remove from the heat. Stir in the margarine and vanilla. Cool completely in the refrigerator, at least 2 hours.

Pour the pudding into the baked shell. Decorate as desired. You can eat as is in a bowl, which is defiantly fun, but I suggest freezing the pie for about ½ hour just before serving so it firms up for a cleaner slice.

No-Bake Coconut Cream Pie

Everyone loves coconut cream pie. And everyone loves no-bake pies (which I like to call "no-brainer" pies). So, this easy, creamy-dreamy treat is a win-win for both harried cooks and hungry guests. The secret is an easy cream filling you make in the food processor. It hardens somewhat in the fridge, thanks to coconut cream and the vegan cream cheese. I like to make this during the steamy summer months, when coconut tastes seasonally refreshing but it's too hot to turn on the oven. Warning: This pie looks innocent, but it's extremely rich, so I suggest cutting smaller-than-usual slices. For the topping, you can substitute Whipped Nut Topping (page 144) or store-bought vegan whipped cream or topping. Or just pretend we're in the South of France and let your pie go "topless."

Makes one 9-inch (23 cm) pie

------

1 All-Purpose Cookie Crust made with graham crackers or gluten-free graham crackers (page 35) or Nutty Crust made with a mix of cashews and macadamia nuts (page 36)

FOR COCONUT CREAM FILLING:
1 cup (230 g) nondairy cream cheese
1 cup (85 g) dried, unsweetened coconut flakes
¾ cup (175 g) full-fat coconut cream
1 cup (120 g) confectioners' sugar
2 teaspoons coconut extract
¼ teaspoon sea salt

1 recipe Coconut Whipped Topping (page 144)

Press the crust into a pan. If making a nut crust, I would not bother cleaning out the food processor before making the filling.

TO MAKE THE COCONUT CREAM FILLING: Process all the ingredients in a food processor until smooth. Spread into the prepared crust and refrigerate overnight before serving. Top with a dollop of the whipped topping.

Coconut Cream

Refrigerate a can of full-fat coconut milk overnight. When you open the can, the resulting coconut cream will sit at the top of the can, while the liquid will sit at the bottom. Scrape up the top to use in this recipe and in the Coconut Whipped Topping (page 144). Some people like to use this luscious cream as coffee creamer.

* Chapter 5 *

Citrus Pies and Tarts

CALL ME CRAZY, but give me the choice between a chocolate and a citrus-based dessert and I'll choose citrus nine times out of ten. Pies made from lemons, limes, and the like are as light as air, yet deceptively satisfying, thanks to tofu and other creamy fillings. These are no-brainers for summer, but I must confess that I often make myself a Key Lime Pie (page 72) or Lemon Fluff Pie (page 73) in February's dead center, the time here in the chilly Northeast when I can't take another snowstorm and am thinking of bikinis, piña coladas, and warmer weather.

Key Lime Pie

This is one of my all-time favorites—so refreshing and so easy. I think whoever came up with this combination—nutty graham crackers against the tart-sweet-creamy Key lime goodness—should be knighted. You can substitute regular limes, but be forewarned: the flavor won't be as pronounced.

Makes one 9-inch (23 cm) pie

---

1 All-Purpose Cookie Crust made
   with graham crackers or gluten-
   free graham crackers (page 35)

FOR FILLING:
1 (12-ounce, or 336 g) box aseptic-
   packaged tofu (Do not use refrigerated tofu; it is too grainy for this
   recipe).
1 (8-ounce, or 225 g) container
   vegan cream cheese
1 cup (200 g) sugar
¾ cup (180 ml) Key lime juice
2½ tablespoons (15 g) finely grated
   lime zest
2 tablespoons (16 g) cornstarch
2 tablespoons (16 g) flour
⅛ teaspoon spirulina or green
   superfood powder (optional, for
   color)

1 recipe Coconut Whipped Topping
   (page 146) or Whipped Nut Topping (page 144) or store-bought
   topping

Preheat the oven to 400°F (200°C, or gas mark 6.

Press the crust into a pan. Blind bake for 10 minutes. Remove from the heat and let cool completely before filling.

TO MAKE THE FILLING: Combine all the ingredients in a food processor and blend until very smooth—better to overprocess than underprocess. Pour into the prepared pie shell, leaving ¼ inch (6 mm) of headspace. Do not overfill. You may have about ¼ cup (60 ml) extra. I usually pour this into a ramekin and chill it alongside the pie for Key lime pudding. Refrigerate for at least 4 hours. I suggest freezing for an hour before serving (see sidebar).

Freeze Your Assets

I sometimes put creamy and citrusy pies and tarts in the freezer for an hour or so before serving, especially during the steamy summer months. It makes it easier to cut a crisp slice. Plus creamy and citrusy pies are that much more refreshing when icy cold.

Lemon Fluff Pie

This is refreshment in a crust. This tart-sweet pie is filled with a creamy, lemony pudding punctuated with happy flecks of lemon zest, topped off with a fluffy cloud of Coconut Whipped Topping. It's a light finish to a heavy meal. Because it's no-bake and citrusy, it's a summer dessert no-brainer.

Makes one 9-inch (23 cm) pie

1 All-Purpose Cookie Crust made with graham crackers or gluten-free graham crackers (page 35)

½ cup (120 ml) fresh lemon juice

1 tablespoon (3 g) agar powder

1 container (12 ounces, or 336 g) aseptic-packaged firm silken tofu (Do not use refrigerated tofu; it's too grainy for this recipe.)

1 container (8-ounces, or 225 g) nondairy cream cheese

2 cups (240 g) confectioners' sugar

1 tablespoon (15 ml) lemon extract

1 teaspoon arrowroot

2 tablespoons (12 g) finely grated lemon zest, plus extra for garnish

Pinch of turmeric, to boost yellow color (no more than ⅛ teaspoon)

2 recipes Coconut Whipped Topping (page 146) or your favorite nondairy whipped topping

Preheat the oven to 400°F (200°C, or gas mark 6).

Press the crust into a pan and bake for 10 minutes. Remove from the oven and let cool thoroughly before filling.

Pour the lemon juice and agar flakes into a small microwave-safe bowl. Nuke for 1 to 2 minutes or until the agar flakes are all dissolved and the liquid is very hot. Set aside and let cool completely.

In a food processor, mix the tofu, cream cheese, sugar, lemon extract, arrowroot, and lemon zest until creamy. It is better to overprocess than underprocess. Add the lemon juice–agar mixture and continue processing. Pour the filling into the prepared crust, leaving ¼ inch (6 mm) of headspace. Do not overfill. If you have any extra, pour it into ramekins to make individual lemon puddings. Refrigerate for at least 4 hours. I suggest freezing for an hour before serving.

Pudding!

You don't feel like making a crust? Make any of the no-bake fillings in this cookbook, pour into individual ramekins, refrigerate overnight, and *voilà*! You have almost-instant creamy vegan pudding.

- Lemon Fluff Pie (page 73)
- Key Lime Pie (page 72)
- Banana Cream Pie (page 60)
- Chocolate–Peanut Butter Pie (page 62)
- S'more Pie (page 63)
- Fluffernutter Pie (page 64)
- No-Bake Coconut Cream Pie (page 69)

Lemon Bar Pie

Give me the choice of chocolate or lemon, and I'll take lemon any day. Lemon bars are one of my all-time favorite treats, so I decided to make a pie of them. Just looking at this sunny yellow pie instantly lifts my mood. Even though this takes a while to bake, you can throw this pie together in under 20 minutes of hands-on time. I suggest using a nonstick pie pan for this dish or greasing your pan well before arranging the crust.

Makes one 9-inch (23 cm) pie

1 Basic Single-Crust Pastry (page 30) or Gluten-Free Single-Crust Pastry (page 33)

FOR FILLING:
½ cup (112 g) margarine
2 cups (400 g) sugar
1 tablespoon (8 g) flour (Gluten-free is fine.)
1 tablespoon (8 g) cornstarch
2 tablespoons (18 g) cornmeal
¼ cup (60 g) silken tofu (Either refrigerated or boxed will work.)
¼ cup (60 ml) lemon juice (from about 3 lemons)
Zest from 3 lemons

Confectioners' sugar, for dusting
Lemon slices for garnish

Preheat the oven to 350°F (180°C, or gas mark 4). Place the bottom crust in the pan and refrigerate until ready to bake.

TO MAKE THE FILLING: Combine the ingredients in the food processor and process until well blended. Pour into the crust. Place on a cookie sheet and bake for 45 to 50 minutes or until the crust is golden. The filling will be boiling, so take care when removing the pie from the oven. Let cool to room temperature and then refrigerate for at least 2 hours before serving. (The pie will set up in the refrigerator.) Dust with confectioners' sugar just before serving.

Pink Grapefruit Tart

My mom loved grapefruits and grapefruit juice. I didn't learn to appreciate this sweet-tart fruit until one day in my mid-thirties, when the grapefruit gene kicked in full force! Now, I can't get enough, When I'm really, really thirsty, I have been known to gulp pink grapefruit juice right out of the container.

Poor grapefruits have been typecast, though, and are not used often enough as an ingredient in recipes. They actually make superb tart fodder. I love the contrast of the slightly sour fruit against the sweet crust. And then there's the gorgeous pink color, which you can "pimp" naturally with a few squeezes of a strawberry.

Makes one 9-inch (23 cm) tart

1 Basic Single-Crust Pastry (page 30) or Gluten-Free Single-Crust Pastry (page 33)

FOR FILLING:
1½ cups (355 ml) freshly squeezed pink grapefruit juice
1 cup (120 g) confectioners' sugar
1½ tablespoons (5 g) agar flakes
4 large ripe strawberries, for color (optional)

FOR CANDIED GRAPEFRUIT SLICES:
2 cups (475 ml) water
1 cup (200 g) sugar
1 large pink grapefruit, thinly sliced
⅛-inch (3 mm) thick

Preheat the oven to 350ºF (180ºC, or gas mark 4).

Place the crust in the tart pan. Line with foil, place pie weights on top, and blind bake for 25 to 35 minutes or until golden. Let cool slightly.

TO MAKE THE FILLING: In a medium saucepan, bring the grapefruit juice, sugar, and agar to a boil over high heat. If using strawberries to color, squeeze the berries, one at a time, over the liquid to extract the juice, taking care not to let any strawberry bits fall in. (Discard the mash.) Lower the heat to a simmer and cook for about 15 minutes.

TO MAKE THE CANDIED GRAPEFRUIT: Mix water and sugar in a large shallow pan or a large stockpot. Arrange the grapefruit slices in the sugar-water mixture. Bring to a boil and then reduce to a simmer and cook on low for 30 to 40 minutes or until translucent, gently turning occasionally with a fork. The rind will fade from bright to muted yellow or pink, depending on your grapefruit. Remove from the syrup. Set the syrup aside.

Pour the agar filling on top of the crust. Arrange the candied grapefruit on top. Refrigerate for a few hours before serving. Drizzle with the reserved syrup.

Chocolate Orange Curd Tart

Chocolate and orange are delicious, humble ingredients on their own, but paired, they scream sophistication. There are several steps involved in making this showstopper of a tart. But the good news is that you can do it in steps—for example, make the candied orange slices and dough one day and the curd the next.

Makes one 10- or 12-inch (25 or 30 cm) tart or eight 3 ½-inch (9 cm) tarts

---

FOR CHOCOLATE PÂTE SUCRÉE:
1¼ cups (156 g) flour
¼ cup (50 g) sugar
⅓ cup (27 g) cocoa
1 teaspoon salt
1 cup (224 g) cold margarine, cut into small bits
1 teaspoon vanilla extract
2 to 3 tablespoons (30 to 45 ml) cold nondairy milk

FOR CANDIED ORANGE SLICES:
2 cups (475 ml) water
1 cup (200 g) sugar
2 oranges, preferably organic

FOR ORANGE CURD:
1 cup (235 ml) freshly squeezed orange juice (from about 3 oranges)
1 tablespoon (6 g) orange zest
1 cup (200 g) sugar
¼ teaspoon salt
3 tablespoons (24 g) cornstarch
3 tablespoons (45 ml) coconut milk or other nondairy milk

Nondairy chocolate shavings for garnish

TO MAKE THE PÂTE SUCRÉE: Pulse together the flour, sugar, cocoa, and salt in a food processor. Pulse in the margarine until combined. With the food processor running, add the vanilla and about 2 tablespoons (28 ml) or more of the milk. Once a dough ball sticks together, let it whiz around the processor eight or ten times. Remove, wrap in plastic, and refrigerate for an hour or overnight.

Preheat the oven to 350°F (180°C, or gas mark 4). Roll out the dough ⅛-inch (3 mm) thick on a lightly floured surface. Cut the dough to fit your tart pan(s) and place in the pan(s). If using a larger tart pan, fill with pie weights and blind bake until just dry, 15 to 22 minutes for a 10- or 12-inch (25 or 30 cm) pan. If using smaller pans, pierce the dough bottom with a fork and bake for 15 to 20 minutes until just dry. Let cool completely at room temperature.

TO MAKE THE CANDIED ORANGE SLICES: Mix the water and sugar in a large shallow pan or a large stockpot. Thinly slice the oranges about ⅛-inch (3 mm) thick and arrange in the sugar-water mixture. Bring to a boil and then reduce the heat to a simmer and cook on low for 30 to 40 minutes or until translucent, gently turning occasionally with a fork. The rind will fade from bright to muted orange. Remove from the syrup. Set the syrup aside.

TO MAKE THE ORANGE CURD: Mix the orange juice, zest, sugar, and salt in a large saucepan. Bring to a boil and let boil for about 1 minute. In a small bowl, whisk together the cornstarch and coconut milk. Whisk the slurry into the juice mixture and adjust the heat to medium-low. Continue cooking over a light boil, whisking occasionally, until very thick and pudding-like, 8 to 10 minutes. Remove from the heat and let cool completely.

Fill the baked tart shells with the curd. Arrange the candied orange slices on top of the curd. Drizzle with the reserved syrup. Chill for at least 4 hours or overnight before serving.

Variation

Substitute lemons or limes for the oranges. If you want something a bit more lowbrow, feel free to make this tart using a nut, cookie, or graham cracker crust, blind baked at 350°F (180°C, or gas mark 4) for 15 minutes.

Double Your Pleasure

Since you're going through the trouble of making the orange curd anyway, why not make a double batch? The extra portion makes a wonderful hostess gift, gussied up in a mason jar with a rustic paper-bag tag. (It's okay if you give them the recipe. Spread the vegan love! Just be sure to spell "curd" correctly.) Citrus curds are delicious on toast or muffins and are reminiscent of orange marmalade.

* Chapter 6 *

Pies in the Raw

BESIDES THE OBVIOUS NUTRITIONAL PUNCH, raw pies don't need any major appliances to get the job done. I created these recipes using just my mini food processor and blender while my kitchen was being redone and I was *sans* stove for more than four weeks. You can make these raw pies anywhere: at a vacation condo, in your dorm room, or in your kitchen.

When selecting ingredients for raw pies, it's important to be extra choosy about quality. The ingredients you purchase are the proverbial stars of the raw pie show, enhanced by some spices and fruit, but that's all. So what you taste is what you get. That said, pick the sweetest blueberries, the crunchiest pistachios, and the freshest spices—and be sure to taste before you assemble so you can make adjustments, if needed. If the blueberries are not as zippy as you had hoped, for example, you can always finish your pie with a drizzle of raw agave nectar to heighten the sweetness.

Just a heads-up: some of my raw pies call for optional, tiny amount of ingredients that strictly raw folks will want to avoid. I've included instructions so purists can stay 100 percent raw.

Serving Size Note

Most of these raw pie recipes make three 4-inch (10 cm) individual servings. That's because I prefer to assemble and serve raw pies in fluted 4-inch (10 cm) tart tins. The gorgeous color-soaked fruits present so elegantly in these simple silver tins; they might even fool your guests into thinking you bought these desserts at a fancy French *pâtisserie*. But if you're of the more traditional ilk, then by all means, make these pies in a 9-inch (23 cm) pie pan. If you do, though, you'll need to double the recipes.

Raw Raspberry Chia-Cashew Pie

The inherent sweetness of the cashews plays nicely against summer's tartest, freshest raspberries. Adding chia seeds to the cashew cream gives the base a pudding-like texture that, in your mouth, parallels the texture of the raspberry seeds. This pie is super refreshing and a great dessert to make and serve on those sultry summer days when it's too hot to turn on the oven.

Makes three 4-inch (10 cm) tarts or 6 mini tarts / For a 9-inch (23 cm) pie, double the recipe.

FOR CREAM:
½ cup (70 g) raw cashews
6 tablespoons (90 ml) water or raw coconut water
2 tablespoons (40 ml) raw agave nectar
Pinch of sea salt
½ teaspoon cornstarch (optional, if you are not strictly raw—helps cream firm up)
1½ teaspoons chia seeds, preferably blond

FOR CRUST:
½ cup (70 g) raw cashews
Pinch of sea salt
4 to 6 medjool dates, pitted and roughly chopped
Scrapings of 1 raw vanilla bean (if you are inclined toward extravagance)
½ to 2 tablespoons (8 to 28 ml) water or lemon juice

½ cup (63 g) fresh raspberries
½ teaspoon lemon zest
Raw agave nectar, for drizzling (optional)

TO MAKE THE CREAM: Soak the cashews in water for at least an hour. Drain.

Whiz the cashews, water, agave, salt, and cornstarch in a blender at the highest speed until smooth (some tiny chunks are okay, but make sure the cream is consistent). Stir in the chia seeds. Let it sit in the refrigerator to thicken for at least 2 hours before serving.

TO MAKE THE CRUST:
Whiz together the cashews, salt, dates, and vanilla scrapings in a food processor. (If you have one, a mini food processor is ideal for this task.) Chunks of nuts and dates should be visible—don't overprocess. Add the water, ½ tablespoon at a time, and whiz until the nut mixture sticks together. Press evenly into tart pans.

Assemble the tarts 1 or 2 hours before serving. Spread a layer of cream into each raw nut crust. Top with the raspberries and an evenly spaced garnish of citrus zest. Drizzle with more agave nectar if you have a sweet tooth. Chill for at least an hour before serving.

Tiny Tarts: The Raw High Tea

Get the girls (and/or guys) together for a raw "high tea." Make a variety of raw pies using 1- or 2-inch (2.5 or 5 cm) tins. Arrange them on a tiered serving dish. Serve on your prettiest flea market china with a variety of herbal teas. And yes, you must drink the tea with your pinky unapologetically extended.

Raw Blueberry Cream Tart

This creamy pie is so decadent that you might forget it's raw, and good for you, and plant-based. Plus, it's a snap to put together. The only reason I didn't classify it as "fast" is because the cream requires at least two hours of chilling time. Make it the night before, if you can. The longer the cream chills, the firmer it will be. Feel free to play around with different varieties of fruits and nuts.

Makes three 4-inch (10 cm) tarts or 6 mini tarts / For a 9-inch (23 cm) pie, double the recipe.

FOR CRUST:

½ cup (50 g) raw walnuts

½ teaspoon cinnamon

Pinch of sea salt

4 to 6 medjool dates, pitted and roughly chopped

Scrapings of 1 raw vanilla bean (if you are inclined toward extravagance)

½ to 2 tablespoons (8 to 28 ml) water or orange juice

FOR CREAM:

½ cup (73 g) raw almonds, soaked in water for at least 1 hour

½ cup (120 ml) water or raw coconut water

2 tablespoons (40 g) maple syrup or raw agave nectar

Pinch of sea salt

½ tablespoon cornstarch (optional, only if you are not strictly raw— helps cream firm up)

½ cup (73 g) blueberries

½ teaspoon orange or lemon zest

TO MAKE THE CRUST: Whiz together the walnuts, cinnamon, salt, dates, and vanilla bean scrapings in a food processor. (If you have one, a mini food processor is ideal for this task.) Chunks of nuts and dates should be visible—don't overprocess. Add the water, ½ tablespoon at a time, and whiz until the nut mixture sticks together. Press evenly into tart pans.

TO MAKE THE CREAM: Drain the almonds. Whiz together all the ingredients in a blender at the highest speed until perfectly smooth. Let it sit in the refrigerator to thicken for at least 2 hours before serving.

Assemble the tarts 1 or 2 hours before serving. (It's fine if you let the preassembled components hang out in the fridge overnight.) Fill the raw nut crusts with cream. Top with blueberries and an evenly spaced garnish of citrus zest. Chill for at least an hour before serving.

Variations

This cream-nut flavor base plays nicely with just about any fruit, so substitute your favorite(s) for the blueberries. Try blackberries, gooseberries, raspberries, strawberries, sliced kiwi, pineapple, or coconut sweetmeats. Or try a combination for a kaleidoscopic raw tart.

Raw Clementine-Pistachio Tart

When I visited the Middle East, I consumed with abandon more than my fair share of their famously cloying sweets. I can still picture those dainty pastries arranged artfully in pyramids and towers, beckoning to me from the sweet shop windows. These raw tarts are inspired by those Middle Eastern sweets; cinnamon, sesame seeds, pistachios, dates, and rose/orange flower water are a classic Arab combination. The clementine topping gives your palate a refreshing counter-balance to the heavy sweetness of the crust. Enjoy it with a cup of fresh mint tea. This is one of my favorite recipes in this book!

I recommend making these as 4-inch (10 cm) tartlettes and arranging the clementines in concentric circles; it looks quite fancy for very little effort. If you're doing the mini tarts, you might only need one or two clementine sections per tart. I like to also use a smallish fruit for contrast/presentation: I prefer blueberries, champagne grapes, or pomegranate seeds if you can get them; lingonberries, French myrtilles (tiny blueberries), or gooseberries would also work.

Makes three 4-inch (10 cm) tarts or 6 mini tarts/For a 9-inch (23 cm), double the recipe.

FOR CRUST:

½ cup (62 g) raw pistachios

½ teaspoon cinnamon

1 teaspoon rose or orange flower water (raw purists, substitute ½ tablespoon orange zest)

Pinch of sea salt

2 to 3 tablespoons (40 to 60 ml) raw agave nectar

Scrapings of 1 raw vanilla bean (if you are inclined toward extravagance)

½ to 2 tablespoons (8 to 28 ml) water or orange juice

3 clementines, peeled and separated into sections (You can substitute tangerines.)

Small fruit, for garnish (see headnote)

Raw agave nectar, for drizzling

A few crushed pistachios, for garnish

TO MAKE THE CRUST: Whiz together the pistachios, cinnamon, rose water, salt, agave, and vanilla bean scrapings in a food processor. (If you have one, a mini food processor is ideal for this task.) Chunks of nuts should be visible—don't overprocess. Add the water, ½ tablespoon at a time, and whiz until the nut mixture sticks together. Press evenly into tart pans.

Arrange the clementine sections in concentric circles atop the raw crusts. Pile about 1 teaspoon of the fruit garnish in the center. Drizzle with agave nectar and sprinkle with crushed pistachios.

Raw Baklava-Crusted Apple Pie

Make this one for your sweeties with sweet tooths ... er ... sweet teeth? The base of this tart is inspired by the flavors of baklava, the famously sinful Greek/Middle Eastern pastry. It's topped with a gorgeous concentric circle of sweet-tart apples, which complement all the flavorings used in baklava, and drenched with a lemon-cinnamon-flavored agave syrup.

Makes three 4-inch (10 cm) tarts or 6 mini tarts/For a 9-inch (23 cm) pie, double the recipe.

FOR SYRUP:
½ cup (160 ml) raw agave nectar
½ teaspoon cinnamon
1 cinnamon stick
1 tablespoon (15 ml) lemon juice

FOR CRUST:
½ cup (62 g) raw pistachios,
    (52 g) walnuts, or (73 g) almonds
¾ teaspoon cinnamon
⅛ teaspoon ground cloves
Pinch of sea salt
3 to 4 tablespoons (60 to 80 ml) raw
    agave nectar
½ to 2 tablespoons (8 to 28 ml)
    lemon juice

2 organic apples (Granny Smith,
    McIntosh, Honeycrisp, or
    Braeburn)
Lemon juice, to prevent browning
Cinnamon, for dusting

TO MAKE THE SYRUP: Mix everything together in a large bowl or mason jar. Ideally you should make this the night before, but let it sit for at least 4 hours before serving so the flavors have time to get to know each other.

TO MAKE THE CRUST: Whiz together the nuts, cinnamon, cloves, salt, and agave in a food processor. (If you have one, a mini food processor is ideal for this task.) Chunks of nuts should be visible—don't overprocess. Add the lemon juice, ½ tablespoon at a time, and whiz until the nut mixture sticks together. Press evenly into tart pans.

Slice the apples as thinly as possible, just before preparing the tarts (a mandoline is ideal for this job), and sprinkle with lemon juice to prevent browning. Arrange the slices in concentric circles atop the raw crusts. Pile about 1 teaspoon of the fruit garnish in the center. Drizzle with the prepared syrup and dust with extra cinnamon. Serve immediately.

Variation

Substitute a ripe pear or an Asian pear for the apple.

Raw Cacao Banana Almond Tart

This one's for the chocoholics. Who doesn't love the hedonistic one-two punch of chocolate and almonds? This also makes an excellent frozen pie. Even raw foodies need a little ice cream pie love.

Makes three 4-inch (10 cm) tarts or 6 mini tarts / For a 9-inch (23 cm) pie, double the recipe.

FOR FILLING:
½ cup (73 g) raw almonds
2 to 3 tablespoons (40 to 60 ml) raw agave nectar, or to taste
½ cup (120 ml) water, raw coconut water, or raw almond milk
4 teaspoons (8 g) raw cacao powder
½ teaspoon finely grated orange zest
Pinch of salt

FOR CRUST:
½ cup (73 g) raw almonds
2 to 3 tablespoons (40 to 60 ml) raw agave nectar, or to taste
4 teaspoons (8 g) raw cacao powder
Pinch of salt
½ to 2 tablespoons (8 to 28 ml) water or orange juice

1 or 2 bananas
Crushed raw almonds, raw cacao powder, or a few raw cacao nibs

TO MAKE THE CREAM: Soak the almonds in water to cover for 1 hour and then drain.

Whiz together the almonds, agave, water, cacao, orange zest, and salt in a blender at the highest speed until perfectly smooth. Let it sit in the refrigerator to thicken for at least 2 hours before serving.

TO MAKE THE CRUST: Whiz together the almonds, agave, cacao, and salt in a food processor. (If you have one, a mini food processor is ideal for this task.) Chunks of nuts should be visible—don't overprocess. Add the water, ½ tablespoon at a time, and whiz until the nut mixture sticks together. Press into tart pans.

Slice the bananas and arrange on the bottom of the tarts. Spread the cacao-almond cream on top. Arrange a few banana slices on top and garnish with crushed raw almonds, a dusting of cacao powder, or a couple of raw cacao nibs.

Variations

- Try substituting hazelnuts or macadamia nuts for the almonds.
- Substitute fresh raspberries for the bananas (divine!). If you're the minimalist type, you can also make this without any fruit and simply garnish with raw almonds or cacao nibs.
- Skip the bananas, for Raw Cacao Almond Tart.

* Chapter 7 *

Nutty Pies

NUT-CENTRIC PIES ARE AMONG THE EASIEST

to make, and they certainly count among the richest. Because they scream comfort, they are a must at most holiday tables, during the winter months, or after a bad day. Add a scoop of non-dairy ice cream—say, for example, soy dulce de leche or chocolate coconut—and you've got instant, full-on hedonism.

The called-for nuts in these recipes are pretty much interchangeable. The results won't be exactly the same, but mixing things up keeps life interesting. And really, seasoned pie bakers tend to be fiercely self-reliant. I find it much more satisfying, for example, to create a pie from ingredients I already have on hand than to have to run to the grocery store at the last minute with a list of hard-to-find foodstuffs.

So feel free to make the Classic Pecan Pie using walnuts. Want to make the Choco-Coco Macadamia Pie, but just can't bring yourself to spend $15-plus per pound on what's been termed the world's most expensive nut? Feel free to substitute pistachios, Brazil nuts, almonds, or whatever other nut strikes your fancy. You can even combine nuts to create your own, unique flavor combinations. If you do decide on a combo, I'll just caution you to make sure all the nut pieces you use are approximately the same size—that is, all nut halves or all nut pieces.

Nuts: Storing Your Stash

Nuts are high in fat, so it's best to buy them in small quantities and store them in an airtight container in the refrigerator or freezer to help keep them from turning rancid. Always smell nuts before using them in a recipe; your nose knows. If your nuts smell like linseed oil, they have probably turned the corner.

Classic Pecan Pie

This pie is an American standby, usually served on Thanksgiving and Christmas. It's rich, gooey, and uber decadent; you can't get any more straightforward than sugar, nuts, and fat, right?

Toasting the nuts is the difference between an okay pecan pie and a kick-ass pecan pie. It's a small step that makes a huge distinction in the flavor and texture, curtailing sogginess and teasing out the pecans' sweet, smoky undertones. I've experimented with all kinds of sweeteners for pecan pies, and I'm happiest with this mélange—brown sugar, maple syrup, agave nectar, and just a splash of corn syrup. Like any ingredient, sweeteners each have their own essence, so this mixture lends more depth and sophistication to the pie than just using straight corn syrup.

Makes one 9-inch (23 cm) pie

1 Basic Single-Crust Pastry (page 30) or Gluten-Free Single-Crust Pastry (page 33)
1½ cups (150 g) pecan halves
¼ cup (56 g) margarine
¼ cup (60 g) nondairy cream cheese
½ cup (115 g) packed brown sugar
2 tablespoons (44 ml) light corn syrup
½ cup (160 g) maple syrup
½ cup (160 g) dark agave nectar
1 teaspoon vanilla extract
¼ teaspoon salt
2 teaspoons orange zest (optional)

Preheat the oven to 400°F (200°C, or gas mark 6).

Roll out the pie crust and arrange in the pan. Place aluminum foil over the bottom of the pie crust, top with pie weights, and blind bake for about 10 minutes. Let cool slightly and then remove the weights.

Meanwhile, spread the pecans on a cookie sheet and toast them on another shelf in the oven while the crust is blind baking. Be careful not to burn; 5 to 10 minutes should suffice. Your nose should tell you when the nuts are done—but check after 5 minutes. Lower the oven temperature to 350°F (180°C, or gas mark 4).

Meanwhile, assemble the filling. Melt the margarine and cream cheese in the microwave. (The cream cheese will not exactly "melt," but heating it will make it easier to work with.) Add the mixture to a food processor or blender along with the remaining ingredients and blend until smooth. Pour the nuts into the pie shell and pour the filling over them. Don't overfill. Save any leftovers to flavor smoothies.

Bake for 55 to 65 minutes. Check about halfway through baking: if your crust is browning (very likely), remove the pie, put a pie guard or foil around the crust, and return to the oven. The pie filling will be bubbly when finished. Remove the foil or pie guard immediately, if used. Cool at room temperature for an hour and then place in the refrigerator and chill overnight before slicing. Serve slightly chilled.

Chocolate-Bourbon Pecan Pie

Indulge all your vices—sugar, booze, and chocolate—in one handy pie. Infused with caramelly bourbon and dark chocolate, this recipe takes the already-decadent pecan pie to an entirely new level of hedonism—but if that's not enough for you, by all means, top it with Coconut Whipped Topping (page 146), nondairy vanilla ice cream, or vegan sour cream. Jack Daniels would definitely approve.

Makes one 9-inch (23 cm) pie

1 Basic Single-Crust Pastry (page 30) or Gluten-Free Single-Crust Pastry (page 33)
1 cup (100 g) pecan halves or pieces
¼ cup (60 g) nondairy cream cheese
2 tablespoons (28 g) margarine
2 tablespoons (26 g) vegetable shortening
2 tablespoons (16 g) cornstarch
½ cup (112 g) packed brown sugar
½ cup (160 g) maple syrup
½ cup (160 g) dark agave nectar
1 teaspoon vanilla extract
3 tablespoons (45 ml) bourbon
¼ teaspoon salt
2 teaspoons orange zest (optional)
1 cup (175 g) dark or bittersweet nondairy chocolate chips

Preheat the oven to 400°F (200°C, or gas mark 6).

Roll out the pie crust and arrange in the pan. Place aluminum foil over the bottom of the pie crust, top with pie weights, and blind bake for about 10 minutes. Let cool slightly and then remove the weights.

Meanwhile, spread the pecans on a cookie sheet and toast them on another shelf in the oven while the crust is blind baking. Be careful not to burn; 5 to 10 minutes should suffice. Your nose should tell you when the nuts are done—but check after 5 minutes. Lower the oven temperature to 350°F (180°C, or gas mark 4).

Meanwhile, assemble the filling. Whiz the cream cheese, margarine, shortening, cornstarch, brown sugar, maple syrup, agave, vanilla, bourbon, salt, and orange zest in the food processor until smooth.

Pour the chocolate chips into the pie shell, followed by the nuts, and then pour the filling over the top. Don't overfill. (Any leftovers make a great smoothie sweetener, coffee syrup, or flavored syrup for pancakes.)

Put a pie guard or foil over the edges of the crust and bake for 40 to 45 minutes or until the filling is bubbly. Remove the foil or pie guard immediately. Let cool at room temperature for an hour and then place in the refrigerator overnight before slicing.

Variations

Substitute brandy, whiskey, cognac, Armagnac, or rum for the bourbon.

Maple-Laced Caramel-Walnut Pie

If you're inclined to decadence, then this is the pie for you. Imagine biting into a crust filled with fresh walnuts, enrobed in a creamy, maple-infused caramel with just a hint of sea salt to counter the sweetness. Serving this à la mode, with a scoop of soy or coconut vanilla ice cream, might just put you over the top.

Makes one 9-inch (23 cm) pie

1 Basic Single-Crust Pastry (page 30) or Gluten-Free Single-Crust Pastry (page 33)
½ cup (115 g) nondairy cream cheese
2 tablespoons (28 g) margarine
2 tablespoons (26 g) vegetable shortening
2 tablespoons (16 g) cornstarch
½ cup (112 g) packed brown sugar
1 cup (320 g) maple syrup
1 teaspoon maple extract or vanilla extract
¼ teaspoon cinnamon
¼ teaspoon salt
1½ cups (150 g) walnut halves or pieces (I like pieces.)

Preheat the oven to 400°F (200°C, or gas mark 6).

Roll out the pie crust and arrange in the pan. Place aluminum foil over the bottom of the pie crust, top with pie weights, and blind bake for about 10 minutes. Let cool slightly and then remove the weights. Lower the oven temperature to 350°F (180°C, or gas mark 4).

Meanwhile, assemble the filling. Whiz the cream cheese, margarine, shortening, cornstarch, brown sugar, maple syrup, maple extract, cinnamon, and salt in the food processor or blender until smooth. Pour the nuts into the pie shell and pour the filling over it. Don't overfill.

Put a pie guard or foil over the edges and bake for 40 to 45 minutes. The mixture will be bubbly. Remove the foil or pie guard immediately. Let cool at room temperature for an hour and then place in the refrigerator overnight before slicing.

Omega-3s!

Most of us don't get enough omega-3s. They lower inflammation, and they're linked to lowered rates of heart disease, triglyceride levels in the blood, depression, and rheumatoid arthritis. Thanks to the walnuts, this pie is rich in omega-3 fatty acids, iron, and vitamins E and B. (I think this helps balance out all the sugar.) Want even more omega-3 love? Add 1 to 2 tablespoons (7 to 14 g) of ground flax or chia seeds to the nut mixture in any of the nut pies in this chapter.

Choco-Coco Macadamia Pie

This pie is super simple to put together, but it tastes so rich and decadent that your guests will think you spent hours slaving in the kitchen. If they remark about it, do not attempt to convince them otherwise. Just shrug your shoulders, and nonchalantly say, "It was nothing, really."

The various raw components of the pie—chocolate chips, crust dough, and creamy filling—taste wonderful as is. So, whenever I make this pie, I end up licking the spatula a little too enthusiastically. You have to taste the uncooked components—chef's reward—but consider yourself forewarned: make sure you leave enough for the pie!

While the pie is baking, your entire kitchen will swell with the aroma of coconut. Don't be surprised if neighbors pop over for a surprise visit. Once cooled and sliced, it's quite pretty on the plate—sort of like a reverse Oreo cookie. This pie is very rich, so cut thinner-than-usual slices.

Makes one 9-inch (23 cm) pie

FOR CRUST:
2 cups (270 g) roasted macadamia nuts
2 tablespoons (26 g) sugar
¼ teaspoon salt (Omit if nuts are already salted.)
3 tablespoons (42 g) margarine
Up to 2 tablespoons (28 ml) non-dairy milk, if needed

FOR FILLING:
⅔ cup (56 g) dried, unsweetened coconut flakes
1 cup (230 g) nondairy cream cheese
¾ cup (150 g) sugar
1½ tablespoons (12 g) flour (Gluten-free is fine.)
2 teaspoons coconut extract (You may substitute vanilla, but it's really not the same!)
¼ teaspoon salt
¼ cup (60 ml) coconut milk (light is fine)

1 cup (175 g) dark or semisweet nondairy chocolate chips

Preheat the oven to 325°F (170°C, or gas mark 3).

TO MAKE THE CRUST: Whiz the nuts, sugar, and salt together in a food processor until almost flour-like. Pulse in the margarine. The dough should start to hold together. If not, add milk, ½ tablespoon at a time, as needed. (Don't bother to clean the food processor.) Press into a pie pan. The goal is to tamp down the crust to about ¼- to ⅛-inch (6 to 3 mm) thick. Use floured fingers or lightly flour the back of a tablespoon to help smooth out the crust. Don't worry about perfection here; just aim to flatten the crust as evenly as possible.

TO MAKE THE FILLING: Whiz together all the filling ingredients in a food processor or blender until creamy.

Pour the chocolate chips into the crust. Pour the creamy filling over the chips and use a spatula to smooth the top. Bake for 45 to 55 minutes, or until the top is just starting to turn golden and the creamy filling is wobbly but holds together. Chances are your nose will tell you when the pie is done.

Let cool completely at room temperature (about an hour) and then refrigerate overnight before serving. The filling will look a bit watery when you take the pie from the oven, but don't worry; it will firm up in the fridge.

"Yo, Rocky!" Road Tart

Please excuse the lowbrow nod to my city, Philadelphia, but hear me out. There's a Rocky statue in front of the Philadelphia Museum of Art, home to the famous steps that the movie character triumphantly ran up. Most people skip the museum's world-renowned art collection (including a gorgeous black-and-white photo by my boyfriend, and this book's photographer, Paul Runyon). Instead, they stand in long lines to get their photo taken in front of the Rocky statue. If they have time—and the energy—most also make their way up the famous stairs where you can actually see an amazing view of the Philly skyline and the Benjamin Franklin Parkway.

Don't get me wrong. Coming from a blue-collar family, I can relate to Rocky's work ethic and tenacity, and I actually loved *Rocky I* (but not II, III, IV, or V). I just think that people need to look beyond the obvious. Enter this tart. Rocky road is more than just a fudge. Now it's fudge with a rich pastry crust. And it's for dessert. This little number looks innocent, but it's rich. If you're not careful, you'll need to run up and down the museum stairs more than Rocky himself did, so cut your slices on the small side.

Makes one 9-inch (23 cm) tart

1 Basic Single-Crust Pastry (page 30) or Gluten-Free Single-Crust Pastry (page 33)

FOR FUDGY FILLING:
1¼ cups (219 g) nondairy dark chocolate chips or buttons
Pinch of salt
2 tablespoons (28 ml) coconut or soy creamer
½ teaspoon vanilla extract
⅓ cup (17 g) vegan mini marshmallows, plus extra for garnish
⅓ cup (48 g) whole almonds, (55 g) almond pieces, or (60 g) walnut pieces, plus extra for garnish

Preheat the oven to 400ºF (200ºC, or gas mark 6).

Roll out the dough as for a 9-inch (23 cm) pie, but create a short-sided tart-type crust, using your hands. (You can use a tart pan if you feel more traditional, but it's much easier to go freestyle for this tart.) Line with pie weights and blind bake for 11 to 13 minutes or until golden brown.

TO MAKE THE FILLING: Melt the chocolate and salt together in a glass dish in the microwave at 50 percent power, stirring about halfway through. This should take anywhere from 2 to 4 minutes, but it depends on your microwave. Add the creamer and vanilla. Stir well and then mix in the marshmallows and nuts.

Spread the filling into the tart crust and then garnish with extra marshmallows and nuts while the chocolate is still warm so it will "glue" your decorations in place. Let cool at room temperature then harden in the refrigerator for about 1 hour before serving. This tastes best served at room temperature.

TartSmart:
Tart

A tart is a pastry base, usually filled with fruits or a creamy mixture, with an open top. Tarts are usually not as tall as pies; most are less than 1-inch (2.5 cm) high, and tart pans generally have scalloped edges.

* Chapter 8 *

Arty Tarts and Free-Spirit Pies

PIES ARE ALL ABOUT STAYING WITHIN THE CON-
FINES OF THE TRADITIONAL ROUND PIE DISH. But
creative types can feel constrained by these rigid, Puritanical baking constructs. Take heart, my pastry-fiend revolutionaries: plenty
of freeform options are available. So go ahead, think outside the
pan, and try some of these pies without borders.

Rustic Freeform Plum Tart

At first glance, plums seem like a fussy fruit to work with—so tiny. But the fact is, because the skin is so thin, you don't need to peel them before adding to pies or tarts. In fact, if the fruit will be visible, the contrasting skin color adds a nice bit of visual interest. Try to buy organic plums, if possible. You can make this fruit tart using any hard fruit, such as apples, pears, or peaches.

Makes one 9-inch (23 cm) tart

1 Basic Single-Crust Pastry (page 30) or Gluten-Free Single-Crust Pastry (page 33)

5 ripe plums, unpeeled, pitted, and cut into ⅛-inch (3 mm) slices

½ cup (100 g) sugar

2 tablespoons (16 g) flour (Gluten-free is fine.)

2 tablespoons (16 g) cornstarch

½ teaspoon cinnamon (optional)

1 teaspoon lemon, lime, or orange juice

Pinch of salt

Preheat the oven to 400°F (200°C, or gas mark 6).

In a large bowl, mix the plums, sugar, flour, cornstarch, cinnamon, juice, and salt.

Roll out the dough into a 12- or 13-inch (30 or 33 cm) round. Place on parchment paper on a large cookie sheet. Arrange the plums artfully (e.g., concentric circles, patterns, lines) in the center, leaving about 1½ inches (3.8 cm) around the outer perimeter empty. Pull the dough up and over the edges to form a rustic crust.

Bake for 40 to 50 minutes or until the crust is golden. Let cool completely before slicing.

Heart Tart for Art

Before my current blog, urbanvegan.net, I ran another blog, which I shut down after my divorce. One of the first recipe contests I held was a "T'Art" contest, and Vicki Hodge, a.k.a. Vegan Vice (Twitter: @Vegan_Vice; Facebook: www.facebook.com/pages/Vegan-Vice, won for her Heart Tart for Art way back in 2006. She created the recipe for her husband Art, in celebration of their then fourteenth wedding anniversary. How time flies! They are now on anniversary #20, and Vicki and I have remained friends over the years. In fact, she has tested recipes for all three of my cookbooks. But the cool thing about good recipes—like good friends and true love—is that they are timeless. This one is easy, pretty, and very vegan. Enjoy!

Makes two 6 x 6-inch (15 x 15 cm) tarts / For a one 9-inch (23 cm) tart, double recipe.

------

8 vegan puff pastry squares or phyllo sheets
2 Fuji apples, peeled, cored, and sliced ⅛-inch (3 mm) thick
2 tablespoons (26 g) sugar, plus more for sprinkling
Juice and finely grated zest of 1 lemon
Agave nectar, to taste
¼ cup (80 g) apricot preserves
1 teaspoon vanilla soymilk
Cinnamon, for sprinkling (optional)

Preheat the oven to 450°F (230°C, or gas mark 8).

Press the puff pastry into tart pan(s) or make the tarts freeform using about 4 sheets each of puff pastry or phyllo.

In a medium bowl, combine the apple slices, sugar, lemon juice and zest, and several squeezes of agave nectar.

Spread the preserves over the crust. Arrange the apple slices in a concentric pattern atop the preserves, overlapping the edges. Build up an edge for the crust, brush it with soymilk, and sprinkle with extra sugar.

Bake for 10 to 15 minutes or until the edges are just golden. Lower the oven temperature to 350°F (180°C, or gas mark 4), cover the crust with foil, and bake for 10 to 15 more minutes. Lower the heat again to 325°F (170°C, or gas mark 3), cover entirely with foil, and bake about 10 more minutes. Let cool. Sprinkle with cinnamon, if desired.

Easy Muffin Tin Pies

Think outside the pan! These wee cutie pies are so easy to make: there's not much rolling involved because of their petite size. Plus, people always go gaga over miniature versions of things. Think bonsai trees, Mini Coopers, and Mini Me, of Austin Powers fame. These pielettes are easily transportable, making them perfect for lunchboxes, picnics, and bake sales. Making them is a great way to use up all those half-full jars of jam hogging shelf space in your fridge.

Makes 6 mini pies; double recipe for a dozen

1 Basic Single-Crust Pastry (page 30) or Gluten-Free Single-Crust Pastry (page 33)
2 teaspoons of your favorite jam per mini pie (mix and match, or not)
¼ cup (60 ml) nondairy milk or vegetable oil
2 to 3 tablespoons (26 to 39 g) sugar, for sprinkling

Preheat the oven to 375°F (190°C, or gas mark 5).

Roll out the dough. Using a 3- or 3½-inch (7.5 or 9 cm) glass or round cutter, cut 12 rounds from the dough. You will probably need to reroll the cutting scraps. Use mini cookie cutters or a sharp knife to cut vent shapes into 6 of the rounds. These will be the tops.

Place one bottom crust round in 6 of the cups of a standard muffin tin. Fill with about 2 teaspoons jam. Don't overfill or it will erupt from your vent like lava from a volcano (unless, of course, you like that kind of thing). Place the tops on and crimp the edges. I like to use a demitasse spoon and a dessert fork. Brush with milk. Sprinkle with sugar.

Bake for 30 to 35 minutes or until the tops are golden brown. Let cool in the pan for about 10 minutes and then gently invert or lift out with a butter knife.

Cranberry Tarte Tatin

With its ruby-encrusted top, this is a gorgeous tart, perfect for the autumn and winter holidays. It looks fancy-pants, but really—truly!—it's a snap to make. If you're feeling adventurous, try substituting other fruits, such as drained pineapple chunks, mandarin orange slices, or blueberries.

Makes one 9-inch (23 cm) tart

¼ cup (56 g) margarine, softened
¾ cup (170 g) packed light brown
  sugar
¼ teaspoon salt
1 bag (12 ounces, or 336 g)
  cranberries
Zest from 1 lemon
1 Basic Single-Crust Pastry
  (page 30) or Gluten-Free Single-
  Crust Pastry (page 33)

Preheat the oven to 350°F (180°C, or gas mark 4). Grease a nonstick 9-inch (23 cm) cake pan.

In a small saucepan over medium heat, melt the margarine, brown sugar, and salt, stirring to combine. Pour into the oiled cake pan and arrange the cranberries evenly on top. Sprinkle with the lemon zest.

Roll out the crust and place this over the cranberries, tucking in the edges. Pierce the top to vent. Bake for about 45 minutes or until the top crust is light golden. Remove from the heat and let cool on a wire rack for 5 minutes.

Trace the edge of the pan with a knife to loosen any dough that might be sticking. Place a large plate over the top of the tart and quickly flip the pan. Before removing the cake dish, tap to loosen any remnants that might be sticking. (This should not be a problem if you use enough margarine and are using a nonstick pan.) Make sure you flip it while the tart is still warm.

Easy Fruit Galette

They say you eat with your eyes first, and because this one uses a kaleidoscope of colorful fresh fruit, your guests will be impressed before they take one bite. The stained-glass window of fresh fruit is an angelically light finish to a heavier meal. It's also lovely during the warmer months or made in mini sizes and served as part of a British tea. This is my favorite kind of recipe: looks labor-intensive, but is ridiculously simple and versatile—don't let the long recipe intimidate you. The filling can be made a day ahead and stored in the refrigerator. For the fruit topping, use a variety of colorful, non-yellowing fresh fruit, such as kiwi, blueberries, raspberries, strawberries, blackberries, or orange sections. Do not use apples or pears here.

Makes one 9-inch (23 cm) tart

FOR PÂTE SUCRÉE:
½ cup (60 g) whole wheat pastry flour

¾ cup (94 g) all-purpose flour

¼ teaspoon salt

4 tablespoons (56 g) margarine

4 tablespoons (52 g) vegetable shortening

3 to 5 tablespoons (45 to 75 ml) ice-cold water

FOR CREAMY FILLING:
8 ounces (225 g) nondairy cream cheese, at room temperature

2 tablespoons (28 g) coconut spread (margarine made with coconut oil) or vegetable shortening

1 teaspoon vanilla extract

3 cups (360 g) confectioners' sugar

¼ teaspoon salt

A variety of fresh fruit, peeled and sliced, if needed (see headnote)

¼ cup (80 g) apricot or orange preserves or marmalade

TartSmart:
Galette

A galette is a French, freeform tart. Everything sounds better in French, *n'est-ce pas?*

TO MAKE THE PÂTE SUCRÉE: In a large bowl, mix the flours and salt. Dice the margarine and shortening and add to the flour, tossing very well so each piece is covered with flour. Using a pastry blender, blend the flour and fats, with the aim of handling the dough as little as possible. When the bits are about pea size, start adding water, 1 tablespoon (15 ml) at a time, sprinkling evenly onto the dough. Use your hands to toss and gently work, again avoiding manipulating the flour as much as possible. (You want to keep the shortening bits intact for a flakier crust.) Repeat until the dough just holds together. If the dough feels wet, you have added too much water. Wrap tightly in plastic wrap. Refrigerate for at least 1 hour or overnight.

Preheat the oven to 375°F (190°C, or gas mark 5).

Roll out the dough into a 9-inch (23 cm) circle, square, or shape into a heart. Or roll into smaller shapes. I like to use a plate or tart pan as a template. (If leaving dough overnight, give it about 30 minutes to warm up at room temperature before rolling.) Pierce the crust all over with a fork and blind bake for 20 to 25 minutes until golden (or about 15 minutes if making mini tarts). You don't need to blind bake with pie weights, but you can if doing so without them makes you nervous. Let cool completely.

TO MAKE THE FILLING: Cream together the cream cheese, coconut spread, and vanilla. Add the confectioners' sugar, about ½ cup (60 g) at a time, and mix until smooth and fluffy. Don't overmix. Gently spread the mixture on the baked crust with a spatula.

Arrange the fruit artfully atop the cream.

Microwave the preserves on high for a few seconds until runny. Time varies depending on your microwave, but 10 to 20 seconds should do nicely. Using a pastry brush, brush the tops of the fruit to seal and prevent browning.

* Chapter 9 *

Savory Pies and Tarts

DINNER CAN LITERALLY BE AS EASY AS PIE once you have amassed a repertoire of savory dinner pies and tarts. All of these recipes are simple and rely on basic cooking and baking techniques. But a few "showstopper" recipes require multiple, yet simple, steps that are time-consuming but worth the effort. Save these for special occasions and for when you need to impress skeptical omnivores. The pie's the limit!

Sun-Dried Tomato Tahini Tart

These elegant tarts make a sumptuous first course for dinner parties or if you are trying to woo that special someone with your cooking skills. Here, I've paired sweet sun-dried tomatoes with creamy-smoky tahini. The tarts can be cut into smaller squares to serve as appetizers.

Makes 4 (5-inch, or 13 cm) tarts

----

4 (5-inch, or 12.5 cm) vegan puff
   pastry squares
¼ cup (60 g) tahini
½ cup (55 g) oil-packed sun-dried
   tomatoes, plus extra for garnish
2 tablespoons (15 g) crushed
   pistachios

Preheat the oven to 400°F (200°C, or gas mark 6). Thaw the puff pastry according to package directions.

Place the puff pastry squares on a baking sheet. Spread 1 tablespoon (15 g) of tahini on each square. Top with a few pieces of tomato and finish with a sprinkle of pistachios.

Bake for 18 to 20 minutes or until pastry is golden and puffed. Garnish with unbaked sun-dried tomatoes.

Aloo-Palak Pie

Aloo palak without ghee is one of the darlings of vegan Indian cuisine lovers. This "reconstructed" version uses all the flavors of aloo palak that you love, in an unexpected pie presentation. It's loaded with vitamins, and it's cheaper than takeout.

Makes one 9-inch (23 cm) tart

---

1 Mashed Potato Pie Crust (page 38)

FOR SPINACH FILLING:
1 tablespoon (15 ml) olive oil
Pinch of nutmeg
1 to 1½ teaspoons garam masala
1 teaspoon black mustard seeds
½ teaspoon turmeric
¼ to ½ teaspoon red hot pepper flakes (Optional, but I use the full monty!)
7 cloves garlic, minced
1 medium onion, minced
¼ to ½ teaspoon salt
12 cups (360 g) roughly chopped, trimmed spinach or baby spinach, preferably organic

Preheat oven to 350°F (180°C, or gas mark 4).

Press the crust into the pan. Set aside.

TO MAKE THE FILLING: In a large sauté pan, heat the oil over medium heat. Add the spices, then the garlic and onion, and sauté until soft, about 5 minutes. Sprinkle with salt if the mixture starts to dry out.

Add one-fourth of the spinach, let it wilt, stir, and repeat until all of the spinach is in the pan. Cook for about 10 minutes. Spread into the crust.

Bake for 30 to 35 minutes or until firm. Let cool for 15 minutes before slicing.

The Dirty Dozen and the Clean 15

Most people can't afford to buy all organic produce; it's expensive. The Dirty Dozen is a list of the most heavily sprayed crops in the United States; I always buy these items organic. On the other end of the spectrum, the Clean 15 lists the least contaminated crops. Check the site occasionally because the list changes: www.ewg.org/foodnews.

Tomato Tart

This is a classic Provençal summertime tart and is best made with the freshest, vine-ripened tomatoes and homemade pesto, though I won't fault you if you use store-bought. Eat this delicious treat the same day it's made. Sliced into bite-size pieces, it's also a fun appetizer.

Makes one 8 x 12-inch (20 x 30 cm) tart

8 sheets vegan phyllo
1 tablespoon (15 ml) olive oil
¼ cup (65 g) pesto
3 ripe Roma tomatoes or other
  small, flavorful tomato, sliced
  ⅛-inch (3 mm) thick
Salt and freshly ground pepper,
  to taste

Preheat the oven to 400°F (200°C, or gas mark 6). Line a cookie sheet with parchment paper.

Lay out the phyllo on the parchment paper and form into an 8 x 12-inch (20 x 30 cm) rectangle (the exact size or shape is not at all important here). Build up the crust edges by rolling the dough under. Brush the crust edges with olive oil. Gently spread the pesto on the phyllo, top with the tomatoes, and brush with the remaining oil. Sprinkle with salt and pepper.

Bake for 20 minutes or until the edges begin to brown.

Variation

Use any kind of pesto or oil-based spread that you like, such as sun-dried tomato pesto, rosemary pesto, or vegan tapenade.

Pesto

Makes a scant 2 cups (520 g)

½ cup (120 ml) best-quality extra-
  virgin olive oil
3 cloves garlic, sliced
2 cups (48 g) firmly packed fresh
  basil leaves
¼ cup (35 g) pine nuts, (25 g)
  walnuts, or nuts of your choice
Nutritional yeast, to taste
Salt and pepper, to taste

Process everything in a food processor until smooth (or smooth-ish, depending on the items you use). You can easily double or triple the recipe. Freeze leftover pesto in ice cube trays or small containers.

Quiche, 10 Ways

Life is short, so shower the people you love with hugs and quiches. Once you realize how easy it is to prepare quiches, you'll find yourself making them again and again. All quiches basically consist of a crust, a cheese layer (which besides adding flavor also serves as a protective layer that prevents the crust from getting soggy), and the custard filling. After mastering this basic formula, you can get as plain or as fancy as you want. This recipe is also a frugal one because you can use what's in season, what's on sale, or even last night's leftovers for the quiche filling.

Makes one 9-inch (23 cm) quiche

FOR CRUST (CHOOSE ONE):
1 Basic Single-Crust Pastry (page 30) or Gluten-Free Single-Crust Pastry (page 33)
1 Hash Brown Pie Crust (page 39)
1 Grain-Based Crust (page 37)

FOR CHEESE:
½- to ¾-cup (60 to 90 g) shredded nondairy cheese (I recommend Daiya brand)

FOR CUSTARD:
1 box (14 ounces, or 392 g) aseptic-packaged extra-firm silken tofu (Do not use refrigerated tofu; it is too grainy for this recipe.)
¼ cup (15 g) chopped fresh parsley
½ cup (48 g) nutritional yeast
1 tablespoon (8 g) cornstarch
¾ teaspoon turmeric (besides flavor, infuses filling with a lovely yellow hue)
½ teaspoon salt, or more, to taste
Lots of freshly ground pepper, to taste
3 tablespoons (45 ml) nondairy milk

For Filling (choose one):

1. **Green Machine:** Use 2 cups (60 g) fresh spinach or kale (134 g) sautéed in olive oil with plenty of garlic and a dash of hot pepper flakes.
2. **Magic Mushroom:** Use 1 cup (70 g) dried exotic mushrooms (e.g., porcini, chanterelles), reconstituted in water and drained very well—should yield about 2 cups (140 g) once rehydrated.
3. **Kinder, Gentler Lorraine:** Use 1 cup (80 g) tempeh bacon, 1 medium onion, and 6 cloves garlic sautéed in olive oil.
4. **Italian Stallion:** Use ½ cup (28 g) sun-dried tomatoes; add ⅓ cup (87 g) pesto to the custard mixture.
5. **Breakfast Quiche:** Use 1 cup (110 g) crumbled veggie sausage, 1 medium sliced green pepper, and 1 medium onion, sautéed in olive oil.
6. **Mushroom-Asparagus:** Use 1 cup (100 g) sautéed mushrooms (any kind) and ½-cup (67 g) steamed or grilled asparagus pieces.
7. **Polka-Dot Quiche:** The name alone will win kids over. Use about 2 cups (260 g) frozen peas or a mixture of peas, corn, and lima beans.
8. **Classic Broc Quiche:** Use 1½ cups (107 g) chopped, lightly steamed broccoli florets; add some red pepper flakes to the custard mixture if you like.
9. **Deconstructed Romesco:** Use 1 cup (180 g) chopped roasted red peppers, well drained, 2 minced cloves garlic, ½ cup (55 g) slivered toasted almonds.
10. **Cheeseburger Quiche:** Use 2 cups (450 g) ground "beef" crumbles layered with 1 small onion, thinly sliced. Add nondairy Cheddar cheese and serve with a dollop of ketchup for dipping.

TartSmart:
Quiche

A quiche is a savory, open-topped, high-sided tart with a custard filling.

Preheat the oven to 400°F (200°C, or gas mark 6). Grease a 9-inch (23 cm) quiche pan.

TO MAKE THE CRUST AND CHEESE: Make the crust and place in the quiche pan. Sprinkle with the cheese. Refrigerate until ready to fill.

TO MAKE THE CUSTARD: In a blender or food processor, process all the custard ingredients until well incorporated, scraping down the sides of the blender or processor as needed.

TO MAKE THE FILLING: Gently arrange the filling on top of the layer of cheese and then spread the custard mixture over the top, being careful not to overfill and making sure that all of your toppings are covered. (If you have any leftover custard mixture, you can make crustless mini quiches: bake for 10 to 15 minutes in greased, single-serving ramekins.)

Bake for 30 to 40 minutes or until the crust is golden brown and the filling is firm. Cool on a wire rack for at least 20 to 30 minutes before slicing.

Booze-Infused Mushroom-Polenta Pie

I realize that using "booze-infused" in a recipe title is not my classiest culinary writing moment. But to be honest, I'm a bit weary of foodies who glamorize even the simplest of dishes. And this dish is simple: honest-to-goodness, stick-to-your-ribs comfort food. This recipe is not difficult, but it is a bit time-consuming, perfect to make on a chilly winter day when you have cabin fever or when you just feel like puttering about the kitchen. It's wonderful with a bowl of veggie soup or a tossed spinach salad. And if you want it to sound fancier, just insert the name of the booze you use in the title, such as "Marsala-Infused," "Sherry-Infused," or "Vermouth-Infused."

Makes one 9-inch (23 cm) pie

FOR CRUST:

2 cups (475 ml) mushroom (preferred) or vegetable broth
1 cup (140 g) cornmeal
¼ to ½ teaspoon salt, to taste
1 teaspoon dried oregano
1 teaspoon dried basil
Freshly ground pepper, to taste

FOR FILLING:

1 tablespoon (15 ml) olive oil
3 cloves garlic, sliced
1 small onion, sliced
3 tablespoons (45 ml) one of the following liquors, in my order of preference: Marsala, amontillado sherry, dry vermouth, dry red wine, brandy
4 cups (280 g) sliced fresh mushrooms (cremini, button, shiitake, or a mixture)
¼ cup (60 ml) nondairy creamer
1 teaspoon cornstarch
2 cups (60 g) chopped fresh spinach
¼ to ½ cup (24 to 48 g) nutritional yeast
Salt and freshly ground pepper to taste

Preheat the oven to 375°F (190°C, or gas mark 5). Spray a pie pan with cooking spray.

TO MAKE THE CRUST: Heat the broth in a large saucepan over medium heat until just steaming, about 5 minutes; do not boil. Slowly whisk in the cornmeal, about ¼ cup (35 g) at a time, to ensure the batter does not get lumpy. Add the seasonings and stir well. Bring to a boil over high heat. Decrease the heat to low/medium-low and cook until very thick and no longer soupy, about 10 minutes. Careful! It bubbles up and can spatter. Spread about ½ cup (115 g) or so in a 6 x 3 x ¼-inch (15 cm x 7.5 cm x 6 mm) layer (give or take) on a sheet of waxed paper. Let the remainder of the batter cool slightly and then spread in the prepared pie pan. Use a small cookie cutter to cut some shapes from the cornmeal layer. Keep it simple: stars, hearts, and circles work best because cornmeal dough can be fragile. Set the shapes aside.

Bake the pie crust for 22 to 25 minutes or until golden.

TO MAKE THE FILLING: Heat the oil over medium heat in a large sauté pan. Add the garlic and onion and sauté for about 5 minutes or until softish. Turn the heat to high, add the Marsala, and deglaze the pan. Lower the heat to medium and add the mushrooms. Cook for about 1 minute, stirring to coat.

Take It Slow!

Are your onions and garlic browning too quickly? Reduce the heat and sprinkle with salt. The salt draws out water and slows down the cooking.

In a small bowl, whisk together the creamer and cornstarch to make a slurry. Add to the mushrooms and continue to cook over low to medium-low heat, stirring occasionally and scraping any bits from the bottom of the pan, until the mushrooms are soft, about 10 minutes. Add the spinach and cook for about 1 minute and then stir in the nutritional yeast and remove from the heat. Adjust the seasonings to taste.

Remove the crust from the oven, but leave the oven on. Let cool for about 5 minutes and then fill with the mushroom mixture and decorate with the polenta cutouts. Bake for 5 minutes more. Remove and let cool for 1 hour before serving, either warm or at room temperature. This is best reheated in the microwave because it helps retain the moisture.

Classic Seitan Pot Pie

These are classic, comforting flavors that just about everyone loves. This is my go-to pie when I'm expecting omnivore guests because it's a "meaty" autumnal filling encased in a flaky pastry crust. Because the filling is dark, a lattice crust (entirely optional) works well with this pie; the contrast highlights the filling. If you're pressed for time, you can purchase store-bought seitan, but making your own is really easy and is so economical (it costs about a third less than in the supermarkets!).

Makes one 9-inch (23 cm) pie

FOR FILLING:

3 cups (780 g) seitan, store-bought or homemade (opposite page)

2 tablespoons (28 ml) olive oil, divided

1 medium onion, chopped

2 medium carrots, very thinly sliced

2 cups (140 g) finely chopped or thinly sliced mushrooms

1 cup (235 ml) vegetable broth, plus extra for water sautéing (if making your own seitan, page 115, reserve cooking broth for this use)

Salt and pepper, to taste

1 tablespoon (8 g) cornstarch

⅓ cup (20 g) finely chopped fresh parsley

1 Basic Double-Crust Pastry (page 30)

TO MAKE THE FILLING: Drain the seitan well (about an hour in a colander). Squeeze the excess water from the seitan and then pat dry with paper towels.

Heat 1 tablespoon (15 ml) of the oil in a large skillet over medium heat. Add the onion and sauté until soft, 3 to 5 minutes, and then add the carrots and mushrooms and cook until soft, about 10 minutes. When the mixture gets dry, add the extra broth for water sautéing, about 1 tablespoon (15 ml) at a time. (You can also add oil, but broth is cheaper and healthier!) Season with salt and pepper. Transfer to a bowl and set aside.

In the same skillet, heat the remaining 1 tablespoon (15 ml) oil. Add the seitan and sauté until browned, about 10 minutes. (Don't stir too frequently or the seitan will not brown properly.) Transfer to a bowl and set aside.

Preheat the oven to 400°F (200°C, or gas mark 6).

Using a fork, mix the cornstarch with the 1 cup (235 ml) broth to make a slurry. Add the veggies and seitan back to the pan and then add the slurry. Bring to a boil and then cover and simmer over low heat for about 20 minutes or until just about all of the liquid is absorbed (it should be moist but not sopping). Add the parsley and stir to combine.

Place the bottom crust in the pie pan. Using a slotted spoon to avoid any extra moisture, fill the crust with the seitan mixture, sprinkle with salt and pepper, then add the top crust, vent, and crimp the edges to seal. Place the pie on a cookie sheet and bake for 35 to 40 minutes or until the crust is golden brown. Let cool completely before slicing.

Homemade Seitan

Make your own seitan and save big bucks. There are as many recipes for this popular, protein-packed meat substitute as there are cooks. After years of trial and error this is my take, but mix and match herbs and spices to make this recipe your own.

Makes a healthy 3 cups (780 g)

1 cup (120 g) vital wheat gluten
1 tablespoon (15 ml) olive oil
1 teaspoon oregano
1 tablespoon (6 g) nutritional yeast
1 teaspoon garlic powder
¼ teaspoon smoked paprika or
   regular paprika
Freshly ground black pepper
7½ cups (1.8 L) vegetable broth,
   divided

In a large bowl, mix the wheat gluten, oil, oregano, nutritional yeast, garlic powder, paprika, and black pepper with 1¼ cups (285 ml) of the broth. Knead for about 5 minutes and then let rest for 10 minutes. Bring the remaining 6¼ cups (1.5 L) broth to a boil in a stockpot. Drop 1-inch (2.5 cm) sections of seitan into the broth, return to a boil, and then lower the heat and simmer for 1 hour. If using for Classic Seitan Pot Pie, reserve the cooking broth.

Pot Pie Marsala

Pot pies are always comforting, but with the traditional carrot-onion-mushroom hearty filling, they can start to feel a bit ho-hum. Here, I've added Marsala—a sweet Italian dessert wine—to tease out the complexities of the 'shrooms. It's amazing how a little nip can elevate such a humble "weeknight" pie to weekend, dinner-party status. You can also substitute a good sherry for the Marsala with the same delicious effect.

Makes one 9-inch (23 cm) pie

----

1 tablespoon (15 ml) olive oil

1 carrot, diced

1 medium onion, diced

1 stalk celery, strings removed and diced

4 cloves garlic, minced

4 cups (280 g) diced cremini mush-rooms (about ½ pound [225 g])

2 tablespoons (10 g) dried mush-rooms (porcini, oyster, shiitake)

3 tablespoons (24 g) flour (Gluten-free is fine.)

¼ cup (60 ml) Marsala wine (or substitute a good sherry, such as amontillado)

1 teaspoon dried basil

½ teaspoon dried oregano

¾ cup (175 ml) vegetable broth

Salt and freshly ground pepper, to taste

1 Basic Double-Crust Pastry (page 32) or Gluten-Free Double-Crust Pastry (page 34)

Preheat the oven to 375°F (190°C, or gas mark 5).

In a large, nonstick pan, heat the oil over medium heat. Add the carrot, onion, celery, and garlic and sauté until soft, stirring occasionally, about 5 minutes.

Add the fresh and dried mushrooms and sauté for 5 more minutes until they start to soften. Sprinkle the flour over the veggies, turn up the heat to high, and deglaze the pan with the Marsala, stirring constantly.

Return the heat to medium and add the herbs. Add ½ cup (120 ml) of the broth and cook until almost all the water is gone, adding the remaining ¼ cup (60 ml) broth if needed. The mushrooms should be completely cooked. If not, add more broth or water and cook until they are soft. Season with salt and pepper.

Place the bottom crust in a pan. With a slotted spoon, transfer the filling to the crust. Top with the second crust and vent and crimp as desired.

Place on a cookie sheet and bake for 40 to 45 minutes or until the top crust is golden. Let cool for about 15 minutes before slicing.

Hash Brown-Crusted Breakfast Pie

What this pie lacks in looks, it makes up for in flavor. This meaty breakfast pie can be made with store-bought vegan breakfast sausage or with tempeh. The fennel seeds give it the slightly sweet licorice tinge you expect from a breakfast sausage. This is perfect for when you are having omnivorous guests over for brunch.

Makes one 9-inch (23 cm) pie

1 tablespoon (15 ml) extra-virgin olive oil
¼ teaspoon red pepper flakes
1 onion, diced
1 green or red bell pepper, diced
1½ teaspoons fennel seeds
1 pound (455 g) crumbled vegan breakfast sausage or steamed, crumbled tempeh (Gluten-free is fine.)
2 tablespoons (6 g) chopped chives
1 Hash Brown Pie Crust, blind baked at 425°F (220°C, or gas mark 7) for 15 minutes (page 39)
1 cup (112 g) shredded sharp non-dairy cheese

Preheat the oven to 375°F (190°C, or gas mark 5).

In large sauté pan, heat the oil and red pepper flakes over medium heat, add the onion and pepper, and sauté until translucent, about 5 minutes.

Add the fennel seeds and sausage. Cook until browned, 20 to 30 minutes, stirring occasionally. The time will vary depending on the brand and whether you're using tempeh or sausage. Stir in the chives and transfer to the blind-baked hash brown crust. Sprinkle the cheese over the top.

Bake for 20 to 25 minutes or until the crust is golden brown.

Mock Meats: My 2 Cents

I'm not the biggest consumer of mock meats, but for meat lovers who want to go cruelty-free, they can be a godsend. But be careful, kids. Just because something's vegan does not automatically mean it's healthy. Some mock-meat brands contain all sorts of nasty preservatives, chemicals, and genetically modified organisms (hence the easier-to-swallow acronym: GMOs). A long list of hard-to-pronounce ingredients usually means it's a Franken-food. At press time, the following brands are the safest bets, made from whole foods: Field Roast (contains gluten), Gardein, and Tofurkey.

Greek Spinach Pie

Think of this as Greek lasagna, with alternating layers of a feta-like filling and iron-rich spinach, enrobed in flaky phyllo dough. It's a humble dish, but everything made with phyllo reads as elegant. Don't let the phyllo fool you—it's easy to throw together.

Makes one 11 x 7-inch (28 x 18 cm) pie

FOR FILLING:
1 bag (16 ounces, or 455 g) frozen
    spinach, defrosted
14 to 16 ounces (390 to 455 g) extra-
    firm tofu
7 cloves garlic, minced
1½ tablespoons (23 ml) lemon juice
2 teaspoons oregano
⅛ teaspoon nutmeg
½ cup (48 g) nutritional yeast
½ teaspoon salt
Freshly ground pepper, to taste

12 to 14 sheets vegan phyllo dough
2 tablespoons (28 ml) olive oil,
    for brushing

Preheat the oven to 375°F (190°C, or gas mark 5).

TO MAKE THE FILLING: Squeeze as much water out of the spinach as possible. Do the same, gently, to the tofu, and then wrap it in paper towels and squeeze out as much water as you can. Finely crumble the tofu into a large bowl and add the spinach and remaining filling ingredients. Mix with your hands or a spoon until combined and crumbly. Taste and adjust seasonings.

Spread a few sheets of phyllo into an 11 x 7-inch (28 x 18 cm) pan. Brush with the olive oil and then top with one-third of the spinach and tofu mixture. Top with a few more sheets of phyllo and repeat the process 2 more times, ending with about 3 sheets of phyllo. Tuck in the edges. Cut a few vents into the pie and brush the top very generously with oil.

Bake for 40 to 45 minutes or until golden brown.

Red Pepper Onion Tarte Tatin

Tarte tatins are culinary wonders, with the tart flipped to definitely and elegantly expose the filling. These tarts are traditionally made from fruits, specifically apples, but the gorgeous patterns and colors in some vegetables lend themselves to savory tatins. I've used red pepper because I like both the flavor and the deep maroon hues, which become more pronounced after you caramelize them. I added some onion for color and to complement the sweet flavor of the peppers.

Many people are afraid to flip tarte tatins. Don't be. Just allow the pie to cool for about 5 minutes after removing it from the oven—but no longer or the caramel will harden. Trace the edges of your tart with a knife, put a plate over the top, and flip it quickly and confidently. If you lose an onion or two, just lift it out of the pan with a fork and replace it, browned side up. No one will know.

Makes one 9-inch (23 cm) tart

FOR TART:
1 to 3 tablespoons (14 to 42 g) margarine
1 tablespoon (13 g) sugar
3 medium red onions
¼ cup (45 g) jarred roasted red peppers, patted dry and chopped
½ teaspoon dried basil
Salt and pepper, to taste

1 Basic Single-Crust Pastry (page 30) or Gluten-Free Single-Crust Pastry (page 33)

TartSmart:
Tarte Tatin

An upside-down tart, it was accidentally discovered at the Hotel Tatin in the 1880s. One of the Tatin sisters accidently put the apples in a tart pan before the crust. She flipped it, and a classic was born.

Preheat the oven to 425°F (220°C, or gas mark 7).

TO MAKE THE TART: Melt 1 tablespoon (14 g) of the margarine in a heavy, nonstick pie or cake pan over medium heat. (I know using a pie pan sounds odd, but it works, as long as your pan is heavy. Do not use glass, obviously!) Sprinkle with the sugar.

Slice the onions across the middle into thirds. You should have 9 rounds showing the onions' concentric circle pattern. Arrange them in a pretty pattern directly in the pan. Cook the onions over medium heat without disturbing them for about 10 minutes. Add a bit more margarine, if needed. The goal is to brown the bottoms and precook the tops.

Using a fork, gently lift one onion and peek underneath to check for doneness. When the onions are browned, fill in any empty spaces with the chopped pepper. Sprinkle the basil over the onions and season with salt and pepper.

Roll out the pastry to fit over the pie pan. Place over the top of the onions and trim or tuck in the edges and press down slightly so that the dough makes contact with the onions. Cut a few small vents using a knife.

Bake for 20 to 25 minutes or until the crust is golden. Remove from the heat and let cool on a wire rack for 5 minutes. Trace the edge of the pan with a knife to loosen any dough that might be sticking. Place a large plate over the top of the tart and quickly flip the pan. Before removing the cake dish, tap to loosen any remnants that might be sticking. (This should not be a problem if you used enough margarine.)

Easy Cheeseburger Pie

Easy, breezy, and extra-cheesy, this stick-to-your-ribs pie will please everyone in your family. It's also a great bring-along dish to potlucks and picnics. This pie is a snap to put together. Making the crust is the hardest part—and you're an old pro at crust making by now. If you're inclined to deca-dence, by all means, go wild and make it with a top crust. Be extra choosy with your broth because this will flavor the pie base. I recommend Better Than Bouillon brand.

Makes one 9-inch (23 cm) pie

1 Basic Single-Crust Pastry (page 30) or Gluten-Free Single-Crust Pastry (page 33)

FOR FILLING:
1 tablespoon (15 ml) olive oil
1 medium onion, chopped
1¾ cups (410 ml) vegetable broth
1 teaspoon dried sage
½ teaspoon dried rosemary
1 tablespoon (8 ml) cornstarch
1 tablespoon (15 ml) soy sauce (Gluten-free is fine.)
Freshly ground pepper, to taste
1½ cups (150 g) TVP (texturized vegetable protein)

1 cup (112 g) Daiya shredded Ched-dar or Jack cheese (More or less, to taste. I like lots!)

Preheat the oven to 375°F (190°C, or gas mark 5).

Prepare the crust and place in the pan.

TO MAKE THE FILLING: Heat the oil in a large skillet over medium heat. Add the onion and sauté until soft, about 5 minutes. Add the remaining filling ingredients, bring to a boil, stir well, and then lower to a simmer. Simmer on low for 45 to 50 minutes or until just about all of the liquid is absorbed. With a slotted spoon, transfer the filling to the pie crust.

Bake for 30 minutes or until the crust is golden. Sprinkle the cheese over the top and bake for another 5 minutes or until melted. Let cool for about 10 minutes before slicing.

Variations
- **For an Indian Pie:** Replace the sage and rosemary with 1 table-spoon (6 g) curry powder.
- **For a Mexican Pie:** Replace the sage and rosemary with 2 tea-spoons cumin and up to 1 tablespoon (8 g) chili powder; start with 1 teaspoon and adjust to your taste.

Pennsylvania Dutch Corn Pie

In memory of Edna Brumbach

I had never heard of corn pie until I was an art student at Kutztown University. There, Mrs. Brumbach, an old Pennsylvania Dutch lady and my then-boyfriend's landlady, served me my first slice, with golden niblets spilling out over my plate. Pennsylvania Dutch are actually of German descent. (Dutch is a bastardization of the word "Deutsch," or German.) This minimalist but tasty pie includes elements of everything that the Pennsylvania Dutch spirit embodies: thrift, simplicity, and efficiency.

Try cutting your vents into hex sign shapes for good luck. This pie is traditionally served in a bowl with some warm milk poured over the top, so try it doused with soy or nut milk.

Makes one 9-inch (23 cm) pie

1 Basic Double-Crust Pastry (page 32) or Gluten-Free Double-Crust Pastry (page 34)

1 cup (110 g) very finely diced potatoes (about 2 small; don't bother peeling)

3 cups (462 g) fresh or (492 g) frozen corn

1 teaspoon salt

Freshly ground black pepper to taste

1 tablespoon (8 g) cornstarch

2 tablespoons (16 g) flour (Gluten-free is fine.)

1 cup (235 ml) soy milk, plus 2 tablespoons (28 ml) for brushing crust

Preheat the oven to 400°F (200°C, or gas mark 6).

Roll out the bottom of crust and place in the pan.

In a medium saucepan, boil the potato cubes in salted water until soft, about 10 minutes. Drain well.

In a large bowl, mix the corn, potatoes, salt, and pepper. Pour into the prepared crust. Sprinkle the cornstarch and flour on top. Pour over the 1 cup (235 ml) milk (don't overfill—you should just see a pool at the bottom of the pie). Top with the second crust. Vent and crimp as desired. Brush with the remaining 2 tablespoons (28 ml) soymilk.

Place on a cookie sheet (it will almost certainly spill—not the prettiest pie, but so good!). Bake for 45 to 55 minutes or until golden. Let cool completely at room temperature and then refrigerate overnight to set. Serve warm.

North African-Inspired Kale Pie

Millet is a wonderful crust base not only because it's nutritious but also because it's malleable and plays nicely with a variety of flavors and textures. In fact, if you are afraid of making pie crusts, I recommend that you start with this recipe. Here, I've paired the millet crust with a garlicky helping of the vegetable darling of the vegan world—kale —along with some raisins, walnuts, warming spices, and a dash of harissa for a North African–inspired savory pie.

Makes one 9-inch (23 cm) pie

FOR FILLING:

1 tablespoon (15 ml) extra-virgin olive oil

5 cloves garlic, sliced

Salt, to taste

8 cups (536 g) stemmed and very finely chopped kale (preferably lacinato, or dinosaur kale)

1 teaspoon dried oregano

½ cup (48 g) nutritional yeast

½ cup (75 g) raisins, soaked in water for 10 minutes, then drained

⅓ cup (75 g) vegan mayonnaise (I recommend Vegenaise.)

⅓ cup (50 g) chopped walnuts

½ teaspoon cumin

¼ teaspoon cinnamon

¼ to ¾ teaspoon harissa, to taste

1 Grain-Based Crust made with millet (see Note) and blind baked for about 15 minutes (page 37)

Preheat the oven to 375°F (190°C, or gas mark 5).

TO MAKE THE FILLING: In a large soup pot, heat the olive oil over medium heat. Add the garlic and cook until soft, about 5 minutes. Sprinkle with salt if it starts to dry out too quickly. Add the kale, stir, cover, and cook until kale is soft, about 20 minutes. Be sure to taste a piece to make sure it's done. Remove from the heat and stir in the remaining ingredients. Taste and adjust the seasonings.

Transfer the kale mixture into the prepared pie shell. Use your spatula to flatten the top. Bake for 20 to 25 minutes until firm. Let cool for at least 10 minutes before serving. Use a very sharp knife to cut. Serve warm or at room temperature.

Note

To cook millet, bring 1½ cups (355 ml) vegetable stock to a boil. Add 1 cup (200 g) millet, decrease the heat to low, and simmer for about 25 minutes or until all the water is absorbed and you can fluff with a fork. It's best to let the millet sit for a few hours, ideally overnight, before using. If the dough is still too wet, add up to 3 tablespoons (18 g) nutritional yeast and mix in.

Variations

- Are you inclined to decadence? Top with 1 cup (112 g) mild shredded vegan cheese before baking.
- Substitute just about any cooked grain (e.g., brown rice, quinoa, barley) for the millet—a great use for leftovers.
- Substitute spinach or chard for the kale. Stove top cooking time will only be 5 to 7 minutes.

Caramelized Onion Tart with Apple-Chile Chutney

Imagine slow-sweetened, melty onions atop a layer of basil-infused cream, topped by a sweet-sour-spicy apple chutney! Although the flavors are complex, the pie itself is simple, but time-consuming, so I wouldn't plan this for a weeknight dinner. Save this one for special occasions, and if you're short on time, you can make it in steps: make the chutney and caramelize the onions one night and do everything else the next. Or make the crust the day before.

Makes one 9-inch (23 cm) tart

1 Basic Single-Crust Pastry (page 30) or Gluten-Free Single-Crust Pastry (page 33)

FOR CARAMELIZED ONION TOPPING:
2 tablespoons (28 ml) olive oil
¼ teaspoon red pepper flakes
3 large cloves garlic, minced
2 large or 3 medium sweet onions (yellow or Vidalia), sliced into thin half-moons
1 teaspoon sugar
1½ teaspoons best-quality balsamic vinegar
½ teaspoon salt

FOR BASIL-INFUSED CREAMY FILLING:
8 ounces (225 g) nondairy cream cheese, at room temperature
6 tablespoons (36 g) nutritional yeast
2 tablespoons (5 g) very finely chopped fresh basil or 2 teaspoons dried

Place the crust into the tart pan, cover lightly with plastic or place in a plastic bag, and refrigerate until you are ready to assemble the tart.

TO MAKE THE CARAMELIZED ONION TOPPING: In a large skillet, heat the olive oil and pepper flakes over medium heat. Add the garlic and cook for 1 minute, taking care not to burn. Add the onions and sauté until translucent, about 5 minutes. Raise the heat to medium-high and add the sugar and vinegar. Let the onions cook for a few minutes and then stir. Keep repeating. Add the salt when they start to get dry; this draws out more water. Take your time and be careful not to burn the onions. If the onions brown too quickly, turn down the heat or add a few tablespoons (28 to 45 ml) of water. Continue to repeat this process until the onions are light brown and taste sweet. (It's a slow process that should take about 20 minutes or so.) Set the pan aside.

TO MAKE THE FILLING: In a medium bowl, mix the filling ingredients with a spoon until combined.

Double Time

Consider making a double batch of the Basil-Infused Creamy Filling. Besides adding zing to this tart, it also makes a decadent dip for veggies or bread and is an excellent sandwich filling. I especially love it on black bread, with sprouts, avocado, and a slathering of the Apple-Chile Chutney. (You might want to whip up a double batch of that, too, while you're at it!)

FOR APPLE-CHILE CHUTNEY:

2 tart-sweet apples (e.g., McIntosh, Granny Smith), peeled and cut into small dice

2 teaspoons red pepper flakes

2 teaspoons lemon juice

¼ teaspoon ground cloves

2 tablespoons (28 ml) best-quality balsamic vinegar

½ cup (120 ml) plus 2 tablespoons (28 ml) water

1½ teaspoons cornstarch

TO MAKE THE CHUTNEY: Place the chutney ingredients in a medium saucepan and bring to a boil. Lower the heat to a bubbling simmer and cook for about 15 minutes. The mixture will start to thicken.

Make a pasty slurry with the water and cornstarch. Using a fork or a small whisk, stir it into the chutney. Cook for about 5 to 10 more minutes until thick. Set aside.

About 15 minutes before baking, preheat the oven to 375°F (190°C, or gas mark 5).

Using a spatula, spread the creamy filling on the bottom of the tart. Top with the onions and bake for 40 to 50 minutes or until the crust edges are golden brown. Pick off any overly browned onions and allow to cool.

Serve warm or at room temperature, topped with the chutney.

Cornish Pasties

This is classic British take-away. These little stuffed hand pies were originally made for workers and schoolchildren to take along for lunch. They are still the perfect lunchbox—or dinnertime—treat, especially in winter when your body demands stick-to-your-ribs food to battle the cold weather.

Makes 6 pasties

1 Basic Single-Crust Pastry (page 30) or Gluten-Free Single-Crust Pastry (page 33)
1 tablespoon (15 ml) olive oil
1 large onion
½ cup (55 g) shredded carrot
½ teaspoon salt
1½ tablespoons (9 g) herbes de Provence
2 tablespoons (3 g) dried parsley
Freshly ground pepper, to taste
2 cups (475 ml) vegetable broth
1 tablespoon (15 ml) soy sauce
½ cup (50 g) TVP (textured vegetable protein)
2 small potatoes, microwaved in their skins until soft
¼ cup (60 ml) soymilk, coconut milk, or oil, for brushing

Have the prepared crust ready in the refrigerator. Heat the oil in a large sauté pan over medium heat. Add the onion and carrot and cook until soft, 5 to 10 minutes. Sprinkle with the salt about halfway through the cooking. Add the herbs, pepper, broth, soy sauce, and TVP. Cook for about 10 minutes or until all the liquid is absorbed. The mixture should be moist, but no extra liquid should be visible.

Roughly mash, smash, or run the potato through a ricer. I don't get too fussy here; no one really sees this. Add to the onion mixture and break up with a spatula as needed.

Roll out the dough to ¼- to ⅛-inch (6 to 3 mm) thick. It can't be too thin or it will be difficult to fill. Cut out 6 rounds about 4 to 5 inches (10 to 13 cm) in diameter. (I have a small plate that I use for a template—measure some of your plates). (A)

Fill each round with about 1 tablespoon filling. Don't overfill or the dough will break. (B)

Crimp the edges with your fingers. Using a knife make slices along one side of the pasties. (C + D) Let chill in the refrigerator for at least 30 minutes or up to 4 hours.

Preheat the oven to 400°F (200°C, or gas mark 6).

Brush each pastie with some milk and then bake for 20 to 30 minutes or until golden. Let cool completely before serving.

Variations
- Add 1 to 2 tablespoons (6 to 12 g) curry powder instead of the herbs and parsley.
- Use mashed sweet potatoes or parsnips instead of the baked potato.

TartSmart:
Pastie

A pastie (a.k.a. pasty) is a hand pie with a savory filling and hails from Cornwall, in the United Kingdom.

Mexican Tortilla Pie

Think of this fun entrée as Mexican lasagna. This cute pie is a snap to put together with supermarket staples and stockpiled pantry goods. It's so easy to make that the kids can pitch in. It's also a hit at parties, so keep it in mind next time you're invited to a potluck. Experiment with different types of tortillas and beans. My current favorite is chile and lime with small red beans!

Makes one 9-inch (23 cm) pie

1 can (14 ounces, or 392 g) black beans, small red beans, or pinto beans, drained and rinsed
1 can (14 ounces, or 392 g) vegetarian refried beans
9 large flour tortillas
1 small onion, very finely minced
½ cup (50 g) sliced black olives
¼ cup (4 g) chopped fresh cilantro
2 cups (224 g) shredded nondairy Jack or Cheddar cheese
1 jar (16 ounces, or 455 g) of your favorite salsa, divided
1 avocado, diced
1 cup (230 g) nondairy sour cream or plain soy yogurt

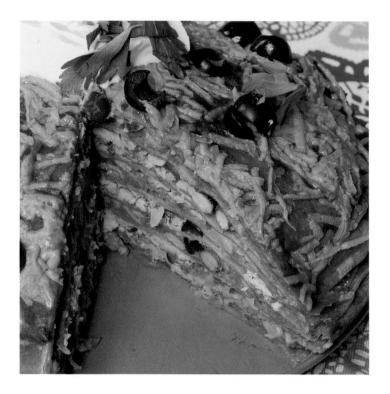

Preheat the oven to 400°F (200°C, or gas mark 6). Spray a 9-inch (23 cm) springform pan with cooking spray. Cover the bottom with foil to keep things clean.

In a large bowl, mash the beans. Divide your beans as follows: refried beans, visualize the can in quarters; canned beans, visualize thirds.

Place 1 tortilla on the bottom of the pan. Spread one-fourth of the refried beans on top then top that with a bit of onion, olives, and cilantro and about ¼ cup (28 g) of the cheese, followed with another tortilla, leaving at least ¼ inch (6 mm) around the edges. Press down in the center. Repeat, using the next one-third of the canned beans. Top with a tortilla and repeat this pattern, ending with a tortilla topping, the last layer. Top with the remaining cheese and 1 cup (225 g) of the salsa.

Bake for about 30 minutes or until the cheese is melted and the pie is heated through. Remove from the oven and let sit for at least 15 minutes before removing the sides of the pan and cutting. Serve topped with diced avocado, sour cream, and the remaining 1 cup (225 g) salsa.

Variation

To make this gluten-free, use rice or corn tortillas. You will have to use a smaller pie pan if you use corn tortillas.

Fennel, Leek, and Olive Tartlettes

These mini tarts make wonderful hors d'oeuvres, and the nonchalant placement of the curving fennel and leeks with the bold black dot of olive makes each square look like a mini abstract painting. These are perfect for dinner parties because they only take about 10 minutes of hands-on time.

Makes 16 tartlettes

4 (5-inch, or 13 cm) vegan puff pastry squares
½ cup (45 g) thinly sliced leeks
¼ cup (22 g) thinly sliced fennel
1 tablespoon (15 ml) olive oil
Salt and freshly ground pepper
16 kalamata or 32 Niçoise olives,
   pitted

Preheat the oven to 400°F (200°C, or gas mark 6). Thaw the puff pastry according to package directions.

In a small bowl, toss the leeks and fennel with the olive oil. Season with plenty of salt and pepper.

With kitchen scissors, cut each pastry square into 4 smaller squares. Place the squares on a baking sheet. Arrange the leeks, fennel, and olives on top of the squares. Bake for 18 to 20 minutes or until the pastry is golden and puffed.

* Chapter 10 *

"Imposter"
Pies

FREUD SAID, "SOMETIMES, A CIGAR IS JUST A cigar." Well, be careful out there, kids, because sometimes, a pie is not really a pie. Observe, and you will find deceitful little food-stuffs lurking in pastry shops, behind prepared food counters, and on dinner tables across the nation, audaciously calling themselves "pies," when in fact, they are actually cakes, casseroles, and pizzas. They are, in other words, imposter pies, or as I like to call them, "sPies." Because they are all damn tasty, I think we can get past the name thing and just dig in.

Boston Cream Pie

It may not be a pie, but we won't hold it against Boston. That's because they have somehow managed to cram three decadent elements into a single dessert: two layers of cake stuck together with a custard cream filling, hedonistically blanketed with dark chocolate ganache. Really, when I am eating this, I don't care what it's called. I only care about making sure there's a slice left for me.

Makes one 9-inch (23 cm) cake ... pie ... whatever!

FOR CAKE:
3 cups (375 g) flour
2 cups (400 g) granulated sugar
2 tablespoons (28 g) baking powder
1½ tablespoons (12 g) cornstarch
¼ teaspoon salt
½ cup (112 g) margarine, melted
2 cups (475 ml) nondairy milk
1 teaspoon vanilla extract

FOR CREAMY FILLING:
8 ounces (225 g) nondairy cream cheese, at room temperature
4 tablespoons (56 g) coconut spread (margarine made with coconut oil) or vegetable shortening
1 teaspoon vanilla extract
3 cups (360 g) confectioner's sugar

FOR CHOCOLATE GANACHE:
¾ cup (131 g) dark or semisweet nondairy chocolate chips
½ teaspoon vanilla extract
¼ cup (60 ml) nondairy milk
1 tablespoon (14 g) margarine
1 tablespoon (13 g) vegetable shortening
⅛ teaspoon salt

TO MAKE THE CAKE: Preheat the oven to 350°F (180°C, or gas mark 4). Grease two 9-inch (23 cm) cake pans and line the bottoms with circles of parchment paper. This is very important to prevent sticking!

In a large bowl, sift together the flour, granulated sugar, baking powder, cornstarch, and salt. (You don't have to sift, but it makes for a lighter cake.) In another bowl, combine the margarine, milk, and vanilla. Using a mixer, mix the wet ingredients into the dry, about ½ cup (120 ml) at a time, and mix until smooth. Pour into the prepared pans and bake for 40 to 45 minutes or until a cake tester comes out clean. Let cool completely and then trace a knife around the perimeter of each cake to loosen before removing from the pans.

TO MAKE THE CREAMY FILLING: Process all the filling ingredients in the food processor until smooth.

TO MAKE THE GANACHE: In a medium saucepan, whisk all the ganache ingredients together over medium heat until smooth and just melted. Do not refrigerate.

Place one cake on a serving dish. Spread the creamy filling on top and top with the other cake, flat side up. Pour the ganache over the top while still warmish, allowing it to drip down the sides. Refrigerate for a few hours before cutting.

Whoopie Pies

Making these pies, which are not really pies, gives a whole new meaning to the phrase "making whoopie." They are American favorites, loved by kids from 2 to 102. Both the cream cheese filling and the cookies can be made a day ahead and stored separately in the refrigerator.

Makes 10 whoopie pies

FOR CREAM CHEESE FILLING:

8 ounces (225 g) nondairy cream
   cheese, at room temperature
4 tablespoons (56 g) coconut spread
   (margarine made with coconut oil)
   or vegetable shortening
1 teaspoon vanilla extract
¼ teaspoon salt
3 cups (360 g) confectioners' sugar

**FOR TRADITIONAL CHOCOLATE
WHOOPIE COOKIES:**

1 teaspoon white vinegar
¾ cup (175 ml) milk
2 cups (250 g) all-purpose flour
½ cup (40 g) cocoa powder
1 heaping tablespoon (8 g) soy flour
   (optional, but makes a denser
   cookie)
1½ cups (300 g) granulated sugar
½ teaspoon salt
2 teaspoons baking powder
1 teaspoon vanilla extract
¼ cup (60 ml) canola oil

TO MAKE THE FILLING: Cream together the cream cheese, coconut spread, and vanilla. Add the salt and confectioners' sugar, about ½ cup (60 g) at a time, and mix until smooth and fluffy. Don't overmix. Refrigerate for about 2 hours to help it stiffen.

TO MAKE THE COOKIES: Preheat oven to 375°F (190°C, or gas mark 5). Line 2 cookie sheets with parchment paper.

Sift the flours and cocoa if you are feeling industrious. (I never do.) Combine the flours, cocoa powder, sugar, salt, and baking powder in a large bowl.

In another bowl, combine the "soured" milk, vanilla, and oil, mixing until smooth.

Gradually add the dry ingredients to the wet, about ½ cup (60 g) at a time, mixing well after each addition.

Scoop 1 heaping tablespoon (15 g) batter per cookie onto the prepared cookie sheets, spacing them 2 inches (5 cm) apart and arranging 10 cookies per sheet. Use the back of a spoon to spread the cookies out to about 3 inches (7.5 cm) and make them as circular as possible because the shape does not change much as you bake. Bake for 12 to 14 minutes or until golden. Let cool completely.

When the cookies are completely cool, pair them off into "twins." (Some will fit together better than others.) Make a sandwich with 2 cookies using a thick spread of filling as "glue." If you are transporting these, it's best to individually wrap them in plastic wrap. And keep in mind that they are best consumed right after you assemble them. Store any leftovers tightly wrapped in plastic in the refrigerator.

Variation

Lazy Day Whoopies: Fill either the chocolate or the pumpkin cookies with softened vanilla or chocolate nondairy ice cream. Refreeze for about 30 minutes.

Pumpkin Whoopie Pies

These are really more like giant cookies than pies. But your guests won't care what you call them. One bite of these rich, autumnal treats and they will surely jump up and down and yell, "Whoopie!"

Okay. Reality check …

At the very least, your guests will smile and let out a quiet but heartfelt "Yay!" These are great for breakfast, with coffee, or as a light dessert. Both the cream cheese filling and the pumpkin cookies can be made a day ahead and stored separately in the refrigerator.

Makes 12 whoopie pies

FOR CREAM CHEESE FILLING:

8 ounces (225 g) nondairy cream cheese, at room temperature

4 tablespoons (56 g) coconut spread (margarine made with coconut oil) or vegetable shortening

1 teaspoon vanilla extract

¼ teaspoon salt

3 cups (360 g) confectioners' sugar

FOR PUMPKIN WHOOPIE COOKIES:

1 teaspoon vinegar

½ cup (120 ml) nondairy milk

1½ cups (188 g) flour

1 heaping tablespoon (8 g) soy flour (optional, but makes a denser cookie)

½ teaspoon salt

1 teaspoon baking powder

1 tablespoon (7 g) ground cinnamon

1½ teaspoons ground ginger

⅛ teaspoon nutmeg

¼ teaspoon ground cloves

1¾ cups (395 g) packed brown sugar

½ cup (120 ml) vegetable oil

1 can (15 ounces, or 420 g) unsweetened pumpkin purée

1 teaspoon vanilla extract

TO MAKE THE FILLING: Cream together the cream cheese, coconut spread, and vanilla. Add the salt and confectioners' sugar, about ½ cup (60 g) at a time, and mix until smooth and fluffy. Don't overmix. Refrigerate for about 2 hours to help it stiffen.

TO MAKE THE COOKIES: Preheat oven to 375°F (190°C, or gas mark 5). Line 2 cookie sheets with parchment paper.

Pour the vinegar into the milk and let it sit for 5 to 10 minutes.

Sift the flours if you are feeling industrious. (I never do.) Combine the flours, salt, baking powder, and spices in a large bowl.

Combine the "soured" milk, brown sugar, oil, pumpkin purée, and vanilla in another large bowl. Gradually add the dry ingredients to the wet, about ½ cup (60 g) at a time, mixing well after each addition.

Scoop 1 heaping tablespoon (15 g) batter per cookie onto the prepared cookie sheets, spacing them 2 inches (5 cm) apart and arranging 12 cookies per sheet. Use the back of a spoon to spread the cookies out to about 2½ inches (6.5 cm) and make them as circular as possible because the shape does not change much as you bake. Bake for 12 to 14 minutes or until golden. Let cool completely.

When the cookies are completely cool, pair them off into "twins." (Some will fit together better than others.) Make a sandwich with two cookies using a thick spread of filling as "glue." If you are transporting these, it's best to individually wrap them in plastic wrap. And keep in mind that they are best consumed right after you assemble them. Store any leftovers tightly wrapped in plastic in the refrigerator.

Shepherd's Pie

It's not a pie. And my plant-based version has nothing remotely to do with sheep or shepherding. Baa! Whatever you call it, this "pie" is a warming, substantial dinner, perfect for chilly winter nights. Because it's portable and keeps well, it's also an excellent bring-along dish for potlucks and parties.

This is a pantry-friendly recipe. Feel free to play around with the potato-topping proportions and use any cooked, starchy root vegetable or combination. You can also use just about any cooked, finely diced vegetable in the filling: great leftover veggie fodder.

Makes 6 servings

FOR MASHED POTATO TOPPING:

1 pound (455 g) potatoes (about 4 or 5 potatoes, exact measure is not essential)

1 to 2 tablespoons (14 to 28 g) margarine or olive oil (see Note)

⅓ cup (80 ml) nondairy milk, for mashing (or to taste)

½ teaspoon salt, or to taste

Freshly ground pepper, to taste

FOR BOTTOM LAYER:

1½ tablespoons (23 ml) olive oil

1 large onion, chopped

4 cloves garlic, minced

1 teaspoon dried thyme

1 tablespoon (1 g) dried parsley

1 package (8 ounces, or 225 tempeh, crumbled

1½ cups (355 ml) vegetable or mushroom broth

¼ cup (48 g) dried lentils, rinsed

1 portobello mushroom cap, diced

1 cup (130 g) peas (Frozen is fine.)

½ cup (55 g) shredded carrot

Salt and freshly ground pepper, to taste

Preheat the oven to 325°F (170°C, or gas mark 3). Grease an 11 x 7-inch (28 x 18 cm) baking dish or medium casserole.

TO MAKE THE MASHED POTATOES: Peel the potatoes. Cut into quarters and boil in salted water for 10 to 15 minutes or until soft. Or leave unpeeled and rice using a potato ricer—infinitely easier! Mash or rice the potatoes with the margarine and enough milk to reach the desired consistency. Season with salt and pepper.

TO MAKE THE BOTTOM LAYER: Heat the oil over medium heat in a large skillet. Sauté the onion and garlic until soft, about 5 minutes. Add the herbs and tempeh and stir to coat. Cook for about 1 minute.

Add the broth, lentils, and veggies. Bring to a boil. Cover, lower the heat to a simmer, and cook for 20 to 30 minutes or until most of the liquid is absorbed and the lentils are soft. The mixture should be slightly wet, not dry.

Pour the tempeh mixture into the baking dish. Top with the mashed potatoes. Bake for 30 minutes. Let cool for about 5 minutes before serving.

Variation

Substitute sweet potatoes, yams, carrots, or parsnips for all or part of the potatoes.

Note

To lower the fat in the mashed potatoes, use just enough oil to infuse a bit of flavor—about a teaspoon—and substitute vegetable stock for the rest.

Macaroni Pie

This is so not a pie, but it holds together like one. This is Barbados's version of macaroni and cheese; it's served practically everywhere on the island, and the English mustard and thyme give it a unique flavor that makes this distinctly not your (American) mama's mac-n-cheese. But it's so easy to throw together using pantry staples that busy mamas—and papas—may put this on their weeknight recipe rotation.

To make this dish gluten-free, use gluten-free pasta (brown rice, quinoa) and gluten-free bread crumbs.

Makes 6 healthy servings

½ pound (225 g) elbow macaroni or other small, tubular pasta
2 small onions, 1 roughly chopped, 1 finely chopped
1 tablespoon (11 g) mustard
½ cup (120 g) ketchup
1¾ cups (425 ml) nondairy milk, divided
2 tablespoons (12 g) nutritional yeast
1 teaspoon black pepper
½ teaspoon thyme
⅛ teaspoon nutmeg
2 cups (224 g) shredded nondairy Cheddar cheese
Salt to taste
½ cup (56 g) bread crumbs (I like panko.)

Preheat the oven to 375°F (190°C, or gas mark 5). Grease an 11 x 7-inch (28 x 18 cm) casserole or baking dish.

Bring a large pot of salted water to a boil and cook the pasta, along with the roughly chopped onion, according to package directions. When draining, immediately rinse with cold water to stop the pasta from cooking further (and turning to mush!).

Meanwhile, in a large bowl, combine the finely chopped onion, mustard, ketchup, 1¼ cups (285 ml) of the milk, nutritional yeast, pepper, thyme, nutmeg, cheese, and salt. Gently stir in the macaroni and pour into the prepared dish. Sprinkle the top with the bread crumbs and then pour the remaining ½ cup (120 ml) milk over the top.

Bake for 30 to 35 minutes or until the top is golden brown. Let cool for at least 20 minutes before slicing. Slices remain more solid if you refrigerate overnight and reheat.

Pizza Pie with 10 Toppings

Who doesn't love a pizza? There's a topping for everyone, and because it's a finger food, it appeals to kids from 3 to 103. But as is the case with dessert pies, most people forego homemade pizzas out of crustaphobia (an irrational fear of making homemade crusts). Pizza pie crusts are actually even easier to make than pastry pie crusts, especially if you use my lazy girl's food processor method. I've included 10 topping options, but in reality, there are probably 10,000, so don't be afraid to mix, match, and even sprinkle a bit of last night's leftover veggies on your pie. There is no wrong way to make a pizza—unless, of course, you burn it. My favorite topping is plain old mushrooms and onions.

Makes one 14-inch (35.5 cm) pizza

FOR FOOD PROCESSOR PIZZA CRUST:
¾ cup (175 ml) warm water (wrist or baby bottle temperature—too hot and it will kill the yeast, too cold and it won't "wake up" the yeast), divided
1 tablespoon (12 g) active dry yeast
1 teaspoon maple syrup, agave nectar, or sugar
2 cups (250 g) all-purpose flour
1½ tablespoons (23 ml) olive oil
¼ teaspoon salt
1 teaspoon cornmeal

FOR BASE:
1 to 1½ cups (250 to 375 g) your favorite marinara sauce, chunked tomatoes, or pesto
2 cups (224 g) shredded nondairy mozzarella (I recommend Daiya or Teese brands.)
Garlic powder, dried oregano, and red pepper flakes, to taste

TO MAKE THE CRUST: Mix ½ cup (120 ml) of the water with the yeast and sweetener. Let it sit for about 5 minutes until it starts to froth; if you look closely, you'll actually see the yeast "burping" up the sugar. It's very important to see the frothing.

Place the flour, oil, and salt in the food processor and whiz to combine. With the processor running, drizzle in the water-yeast mixture through the processor funnel until combined. Then with the blade still running, drizzle in just enough of the remaining ¼ cup (60 ml) water to form a unified dough ball. When you have a dough ball, whiz it around about 20 or so times.

Spray a large bowl with cooking spray. Remove the dough, place in the oiled bowl, cover, and let rise in a warm, draft-free place for 15 minutes. (Now is a good time to prepare your pizza toppers: slice and sauté, what have you.)

Preheat the oven to 425°F (220°C, or gas mark 7). Spray a pizza pan lightly with cooking spray and toss on the cornmeal to prevent sticking.

Stretch out the dough with your hands and pat into the pan. Stretch to your desired thickness (I prefer a thin crust), keeping in mind that the crust size will just about double after baked.

TO MAKE THE BASE: With a ladle, spread your sauce evenly on top of the dough. Top with the cheese, then the toppings, followed by the seasonings, and bake for about 15 minutes until the cheese is melted and the crust is lightly browned. Here's the hardest part: let cool for about 10 minutes before slicing.

10 Topping Ideas (choose one):

1. **White Pizza:** Skip the marinara sauce. Sprinkle cheese directly on the crust. Sprinkle about 3 cloves crushed garlic over the sauce and top with about 1½ cups (107 g) cooked broccoli.

2. **Exotic Truffled Mushroom:** Sauté 2 cups (140 g) exotic mushrooms in some olive oil and garlic until soft. Transfer to your pie with a slotted spoon and bake. Finish with a drizzle of truffle oil.

3. **Pesto-licious:** Before baking, top cheese with dollops of pesto and a few handfuls of pine nuts.

4. **Arugula:** This is classic Italian. Prepare the pie as described above and then top the freshly baked pizza with 4 cups (80 g) fresh arugula. Delicious!

5. **Faux-Meat Head:** Top pie with your favorite faux meat. Please use only products of which you can pronounce the ingredients—no Frankenfoods allowed—such as sausage crumbles, ground "beef" crumbles, or tempeh bacon.

6. **Carb Lovers' Pizza Pie:** Slice 1 large potato very thinly with a mandoline. Pat dry and sauté in a medium nonstick pan in 1 teaspoon olive oil and 1 teaspoon of your favorite dried herb (e.g., basil, thyme, rosemary). Scatter on top of cheese before baking.

7. **Quattro Stagione** (four seasons, 1 quarter of each pie for each "season"): After cheese, place one of each of the following on one-fourth of the pie: ½ cup (70 g) sliced green and black olives; ½ cup (90 g) drained, chopped roasted red peppers; ½ cup (150 g) drained artichoke hearts; 1 cup (34 g) finely chopped kale.

8. **Flyin' Hawaiian** (named for my favorite former Phillie, Shane Victorino): Use Jack cheese. Top with ⅓ cup (55 g) cubed pineapple, ½ cup (40 g) chopped tempeh bacon, and ¼ cup (25 g) finely chopped scallion.

9. **Italian Flag:** In a large skillet, sauté 3 cloves minced garlic in 1 teaspoon olive oil. Add 2 cups (60 g) fresh spinach and cook over medium heat until just wilted. Scatter atop cheese, and top that with about ⅓ cup (37 g) drained sun-dried tomatoes.

10. **Mexi-Pizza:** Use salsa instead of marinara and use Jack cheese. Top with 1 cup (240 g) drained black beans, ¼ cup (25 g) chopped scallion, and 1 cup (110 g) crumbled veggie chorizo. After the pie is baked, you can add some fresh cilantro and chopped fresh avocado, if you like.

* Chapter 11 *

Pie
Toppers

DON'T GET ME WRONG: A WELL-PREPARED PIE IS PERFECTLY RESPECTABLE ON ITS OWN, save for perhaps a cup of tea or coffee on the side. A good pie should need no additional adornments. But I'm the kind of girl who loves to accessorize! Pimping your pie with drizzles of sauces, dollops of cream, or even a humble scoop of nondairy ice cream is an easy and fun way to elevate your creations to new levels of delicious-ness and decadence. Serving pies with various sauces and other accessories can also tease out certain flavor qualities. For example, my nutty whipped toppings help balance cloyingly sweet pies and infuse them with a sense of gravitas and sophistication. These pie topper recipes allow you plenty of room for improvisation. Think of them as springboards to your culinary creativity!

Whipped Nut Topping and 10 Variations

This light, creamy topping is the austere counterpoint to the cloying sweetness of the Chocolate-Bourbon Pecan Pie (page 90). Serve a dollop on the side with this pie or any other pie. Confession: I sometimes make this cream solo and eat it as a pudding for breakfast or dessert. So don't toss the leftovers!

Makes about 1 cup (235 ml)

½ cup (70 g) raw cashews
½ cup (50 g) raw walnuts
1 tablespoon (8 g) cornstarch
¾ cup (175 ml) nondairy milk
1 to 3 tablespoons (20 to 60 g)
  maple syrup or agave nectar

Good Libations

Some alcoholic beverages contain dairy while others are clarified with animal products. Not sure if your liquor is vegan? Look it up on barnivore.com.

Soak the nuts in water to cover for at least an hour. Drain.

Whiz the nuts, cornstarch, and milk in a blender at the highest speed until perfectly smooth. Add the sweetener, 1 tablespoon (20 g) at a time, to taste. Refrigerate overnight before serving. (You can serve immediately but it won't be totally thickened.)

10 Variations

To create variations, add the following ingredients when whizzing the mixture in the blender:

1. **Chocolate:** Add 2 tablespoons (10 g) cocoa powder.
2. **Caramel:** Add 3 or 4 vegan caramels melted in the microwave on 50 percent power.
3. **Vanilla:** Add 2 teaspoons vanilla extract and the scrapings from 1 vanilla bean. (Don't throw the stem away! Put it in your sugar container to infuse your sugar with a yummy vanilla essence.)
4. **Peanut Butter:** Add 2 tablespoons (32 g) creamy peanut butter.
5. **Maple:** Add 1½ teaspoons maple extract.
6. **Sesame:** Add 2 tablespoons (30 g) tahini.
7. **Horchata:** Replace cashews with almonds and add ½ teaspoon cinnamon.
8. **Boozy:** Add 2 to 3 tablespoons (28 to 45 ml) of your favorite cream-flavor-compatible liqueur, such as Kahlua, amaretto, rum, brandy, cognac, or whiskey.
9. **Coffee:** Dissolve 1 tablespoon (3 g) instant coffee granules in about 2 or 3 tablespoons (28 to 45 ml) of the milk and then whiz with remaining ingredients in blender. Add a shot of Kahlua if you're inclined toward decadence (and don't have an issue with caffeine).
10. **Chocolate-Hazelnut:** Add 2 tablespoons (32 g) vegan chocolate-hazelnut spread (available in most health food stores).

Coconut Whipped Topping

This topping is a little dollop of heaven. It's integral to a few pies, like Banana Cream Pie (page 60), but it's also wonderful atop a fruit pie and is a must-serve over Pumpkin Pie (page 53) on Thanksgiving. You need full-fat coconut milk for this decadent topping. Besides, if you're going to splurge on whipped topping, you may as well do the full Monty. This will not whip into the stiff peaks you get with dairy whipped cream.

Makes about 1 cup (235 ml); double the recipe if using to top an entire pie; triple the recipe if you are greedy, like me

----

1 can (14 ounces, or 392 g) full-fat coconut milk, refrigerated for at least 12 hours
¼ to ⅓ cup (30 to 40 g) confectioners' sugar (sweeten to your taste)
Pinch of salt
½ teaspoon vanilla extract

Chill Out

Before making this whipped topping, it's important to chill your metal bowl and beaters in the freezer for at least 30 minutes. The colder the ingredients, the thicker the whipped topping.

If you refrigerate the coconut milk long enough, the fatty part (which we are using) will separate from the liquid. Using a spoon, scoop out the white, fatty part and place in a stainless steel bowl. Alternatively, pierce holes in the top of the can and gently pour out the clear liquid. (Save the liquid for smoothies!) Then open the can and scoop out the white fatty part.

Using a mixer or a wire whisk, whip until fluffy. Don't overmix or you'll end up with sauce.

Add the confectioners' sugar, about 1 tablespoon (8 g) at a time, and whip in until combined. Fold in the salt and vanilla. Serve immediately. Or refrigerate, covered, until serving—but only for a few hours; this topping works best when freshly made.

Coconut Dulce de Leche

A South American classic, this gooey, caramelly sauce is usually made with dairy milk and is especially popular in Buenos Aires. I've put a plant-based twist on it using coconut cream. Let's face it: anything with coconut cream is dreamy-creamy good. Coconut Dulce de Leche is a muy decadent pie topper, and if you have any left over, it's fabulous atop sundaes or swirled into your tea.

Makes 1 heaping cup (235 ml)

1 cup (235 g) coconut cream (see sidebar, page 144)
1 tablespoon (14 g) margarine
1 cup (225 g) packed dark brown sugar
¼ teaspoon salt
½ cup (120 ml) nondairy milk
1 teaspoon vanilla extract

Bring all the ingredients to a boil in a medium saucepan. Watching carefully so it does not spill over, boil for 7 to 8 minutes, then reduce the heat to low, and boil very gently for about 30 minutes or until the sauce is reduced by half. Allow to cool. You can store tightly covered at room temperature if you'll be using it up in the next few days. If not, then store in an airtight container in the refrigerator for up to 2 weeks. Bring to room temperature before using—the fat in the coconut cream will harden and bringing it to room temperature will "melt" them.

1. Water versus cream in coconut milk
2. Process
3. Finished product

Butterscotch Sauce

This is a classic when it comes to ice cream, and you can certainly use this recipe to make a sundae topper. But I think caramelly butterscotch sauce adds a wonderful earthy sweetness to many pies—think apple, pumpkin, parsnip, and most nut pies. Being a minimalist cook, I never use a candy thermometer to make mine. I just watch until the sauce sticks to the back of the spoon.

Makes about 1 cup (235 ml)

1 cup (225 g) packed brown sugar
¼ cup (60 ml) nondairy milk
1 teaspoon vanilla extract
3 tablespoons (42 g) margarine
¼ teaspoon salt

Mix everything in a medium saucepan and bring to a boil. Lower the heat and gently simmer for about 10 minutes. Refrain from stirring too often! Once the sauce sticks to the back of your spoon, it's done. Turn off the heat and let the pan sit on the burner until the liquid is cool.

Chocolate Sauce

I like to call this silky sauce my LCS, or the chocolate or creamy pie's equivalent to the little black dress (LBD). Sure, you can buy it, but it's simple to put together, and you can control the quality of the cocoa. Drizzle, splatter, and douse with abandon! Use any leftovers to top sundaes or make chocolate milk. To this end, you may want to whip up a double batch.

Makes about 1 ½ cups (355 ml)

1 cup (200 g) sugar

½ cup (40 g) cocoa powder

Pinch of salt

1 teaspoon vanilla extract

½ cup (88 g) best-quality nondairy
chocolate chips, buttons, or
chunks

2 teaspoons cornstarch

Combine the sugar, cocoa, salt, and vanilla in a medium saucepan and bring to a boil. Let it cook at a rolling boil for about 3 minutes, stirring occasionally. Lower the heat to medium-low and cook for 5 minutes more, stirring occasionally. Add the chocolate and stir until melted. Sprinkle in the cornstarch, a tiny bit at a time, and whisk until smooth. Remove from the heat. Let sit until cool. Store in the refrigerator, where it will thicken.

Variation

Mocha: Add 1 teaspoon instant espresso powder or instant coffee.

* Resources *

Bob's Red Mill

www.bobsredmill.com

Bob's Red Mill offers packaged and bulk stone-ground whole-grain and natural foods in small or large quantities. It's a great resource for gluten-free and unusual flours.

Fante's

www.fantes.com

Fante's offers an incredibly well-stocked bakeshop, with all kinds of pie-baking accoutrements, located in the heart of Philadelphia's famous Italian Market.

King Arthur Flour Company

www.kingarthurflour.com

This company offers top-quality flours, tools, equipment, and specialty items. The site also includes some vegan recipes.

Kitchen Krafts

www.kitchenkrafts.com

Kitchen Krafts offers a dizzying array of baking equipment, gadgets, and ingredients, including plenty of gluten-free supplies—from highbrow to lowbrow.

Sur La Table

www.surlatable.com

Sur La Table offers a bevy of baking supplies, cookbooks, and serving options—available both online and in retail stores. If shopping online, be sure to check out their sale section.

Vegan Essentials

www.veganessentials.com

This is the full vegan monty—especially useful if you do not live in close proximity to a city or a well-stocked natural foods store. They offer a complete array of easy- and harder-to-find vegan foodstuffs, including vegan canned whipped creams, marshmallows and marshmallow fluff, chocolate chips, and pantry essentials. I've been ordering from them for years and they are great. Be sure to register because they offer coupon deals from time to time.

Williams-Sonoma

www.williams-sonoma.com

Williams-Sonoma offers upscale baking equipment and ingredients—available both online and in retail stores.

* *Acknowledgments* *

I HAVE SO MANY PEOPLE TO THANK:

First, to my sweetie pie—and pie photographer—Paul Runyon. Each day, I feel thankful we somehow found each other in this big, crazy world. I love you. XOXO

To my family, for supporting me and believing in me. Special big hugs and thanks to two amazing women and role models, my beautiful aunts, Cioci Regina and Cioci Genia. Your encouragement and positivity over the years have helped me more than you'll ever know.

What would I do without my girlfriends? Mille mercis: Violet Phillips, Karen Pearlman, Ann Duffield, Claire Nixon, and Stacey Saleff.

My agent, Clare Pelino, for her support, go-get-'em-ness, and encouragement.

The folks at Quarry: What a wonderful, organized, and encouraging team! It has been a pleasure to work with you.

To Bruce Wartman, for being a friend and for making my dream kitchen a reality.

Kudos to my few, handpicked recipe testers: Carrie Horsburgh Bagnell, Liz Wyman, Margo Marmon, and Karen Teig.

And to my recipe tasters: Bruce and Lynne Wartman; Dr. Ali Horowitz; Jeremy Shabtai; and Ann, Tim, Gareth and Mena Duffield.

To my blog readers: Your positivity and good energy keep me motivated.

To the folks at Digitas, for continuing to be so supportive and fabulous!

To the brilliant Dr. Richard Shlansky-Goldberg and Dr. Samantha Pfieffer. Thank you for restoring my health!

* *About the Author* *

Dynise Balcavage is the author of two additional plant-based cookbooks, *The Urban Vegan* and *Celebrate Vegan*, and her cruelty-free recipes have appeared in *VegNews, Vegetarian Times, Philadelphia Daily News*, and *Végétariens* magazine (in French). Dynise has been interviewed in the *New York Times* and the *International Herald Tribune* and has done cooking demonstrations from New York to Paris. She lives in Philly with her two former alley cats, blogs at urbanvegan.net, and tweets at theurbanvegan.

* *About the Photographer* *

Paul Runyon's current work centers on how the masses interface with the contemporary American Western landscape and its accompanying complexities, contradictions, and ambiguities.

Runyon's photographs are held in collections in the National Portrait Gallery in Washington, D.C.; the Philadelphia Museum of Art; the United States Information Agency in Washington, D.C.; the Frank Goodyear Collection; and the Mellon Bank Corporate Collection. His work was recently included in the exhibition "Streets of Philadelphia: Photography 1970–1985," the first overview of street photography made in Philadelphia during the 1970s and '80s.

Runyon has been a professor of photography at Philadelphia's Drexel University since 1993 and has chaired the university's Photography Program for the past decade. In addition to his fine art career, numerous Fortune 500 companies, including AT&T, Arm & Hammer, Citicorp Bank, IBM, and Nissan, have commissioned Runyon's photography. He divides his time between Philadelphia; Tucson, Arizona; and Torrey, Utah. You can view his work at paulrunyon.com.

pie vents, 20
pie weights, 20, 21
pistachios
    raw clementine-pistachio tart, 82
pizza pie, 140–141
plum tart, rustic freeform, 98
polenta
    booze-infused mushroom-polenta
        pie, 112–113
polka-dot quiche, 110
potatoes
    carb lovers' pizza, 141
    hash brown pie crust, 39
    mashed potato pie crust, 38
    shepherd's pie, 138
prebaking, 32
pudding, 73
puff pastry, 16
pumpkin
pumpkin pie, 53
pumpkin whoopie pies, 137

Q

quattro stagione pizza, 141
quiche, 110–111

R

raspberries
    nectarine-raspberry pie, 50
    raw raspberry chia-cashew pie, 80
raw pies, 79
    blueberry cream tart, 81
    cacao banana almond tart, 84
    clementine-pistachio tart, 82
    raspberry chia-cashew pie, 80

raw baklava-crusted apple pie, 83
    serving sizes, 79
red pepper onion tarte tatin, 121
resources, 151
rhubarb pie, strawberry-, 48
Ricemellow Creme, 63
rolling pins, 18

S

salt, 16, 17
sauces
    butterscotch sauce, 148
    chocolate sauce, 149
savory pies and tarts, 105
    aloo-palak pie, 107
    booze-infused mushroom-polenta
        pie, 112–113
    caramelized onion tart with apple-
        chile chutney, 126–127
    classic seitan pot pie, 114
    Cornish pastie, 128–129
    easy cheeseburger pie, 122
    fennel, leek, and olive tartlettes, 131
    Greek spinach pie, 118
    hash brown-crusted breakfast pie, 117
    Mexican tortilla pie, 130
    North African-inspired kale pie, 124
    Pennsylvania Dutch corn pie, 123
    pot pie Marsala, 116
    quiche, 110–111
    red pepper onion tarte tatin, 121
    sun-dried tomato tahini tart, 106
    tomato tart, 108
sea salt, 16, 17
seitan
    classic seitan pot pie, 114

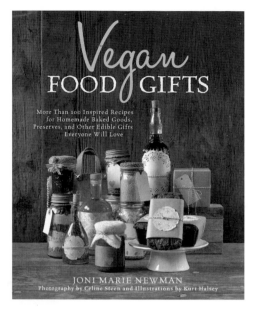

Vegan Food Gifts
ISBN: 978-1-59233-529-9

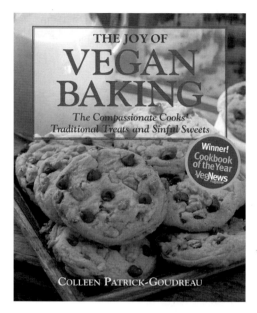

The Joy of Vegan Baking
ISBN: 978-1-59233-280-9

Great Gluten-Free Vegan Eats
ISBN: 978-1-59233-513-8

Whole Grain Vegan Baking
ISBN: 978-1-59233-545-9